SPORTS

& RECREATIONAL FACILITIES

SPORTS
& RECREATIONAL FACILITIES

Roger Yee

Visual Reference Publications, Inc.

Left: Citizens Bank Park
Philadelphia, Pennsylvania.

Design firm: EwingCole.

Photographer: Jeffrey Totaro.

Visual Reference Publications, Inc.
302 Fifth Avenue
New York, NY 10001

Distributors to the trade in the United States and Canada:
Watson-Guptill
770 Broadway
New York, NY 10003

Distributors outside the United States and Canada:
HarperCollins International
10 East 53rd Street
New York, NY 10022-5299

Book design: Veronika Cherepanina

Library of Congress Cataloging in Publication Data:
Sports & Recreational Facilities

ISBN 1-58471-083-7

Printed in China

CONTECTS

Introduction by Roger Yee   5

ARC/Architectural Resources Cambridge, Inc.   9

Barker Rinker Seacat Architecture, P.C.   17

Cannon Design   25

Dattner Architects   33

David M. Schwarz / Architectural Services, Inc.   41

ELS   49

EwingCole   57

Hastings & Chivetta Architects, Inc.   73

Hughes Group Architects   89

Jack L. Gordon Architects, PC AIA   97

Mojo • Stumer Architects   105

Rossetti   113

Sasaki Associates Inc.   121

Souto Moura Arquitectos Lda   129

Editorial: The Day When Everybody Wins   137

NIRSA Outstanding Sports Facilities Awards   143

Index by Project   192

Left: Johns Hopkins University
Ralph S.O'Connor Recreation Center.
Baltimore, Maryland.

Design firm: Sasaki Associates, Inc.

Introduction

Run for Your Life

Who's really tough when the tough get going? Sure, the NFL's Green Bay Packers are tough. But so are Packers fans. Even though Lambeau Field, the Packers' 72,601-seat home in Green Bay, Wisconsin, has been continuously improved since opening in 1957 to give fans extra seating, concession stands and toilets, new event facilities, and the five-story, 366,000-square-foot Lambeau Field Atrium, featuring the Packers Pro Shop, Packers Hall of Fame, and numerous restaurants, football is still played outdoors. In Green Bay, that means assembling at the site of the infamous "Ice Bowl" of December 31, 1967, when the Packers overpowered the Dallas Cowboys to take the NFL title, and the temperature plunged to 13 degrees below zero.

Still, things are looking up for sports fans and athletes, and not just in Green Bay. The newest stadiums, recreational centers and other sports venues are designed to benefit spectators and non-athletes as well as athletes and staff. With sports competing for attention in an age when leisure activity is big business, the focus in sports architecture has shifted from complying with the rules and regulations of sports to the comfort, safety and convenience of people at sports events. Sports now represent social events where the action extends from the field to shops, restaurants, sports museums and more.

Nor are athletes the only people in a sweat. New recreational facilities welcome amateurs and non-athletes who know they're not the next Barry Bonds or Lindsay Davenport, but like to keep fit and have fun. What do they want to do? Many choose basketball, swimming and other traditional activities. However, there's growing interest in yoga, spinning and other new pursuits, so new buildings also pay attention to them. If physical activity is vital to physical and mental fitness for people of all ages, developers of sports facilities will eagerly appeal to them.

Architecture completes this picture of athletic talent, holistic wellness and social gathering in innovative ways that were not imagined as recently as two decades ago. Today's sports facilities construct a total experience for sports, shaping the space around each activity to enhance its effectiveness, safety, pleasure, and even meaning, in the larger context of modern life. That's evident in the noteworthy projects on the following pages, which are supplemented by the prestigious Outstanding Sports Facilities Awards of The National Intramural-Recreational Sports Association. Take a look, Packers fans.

Roger Yee
Editor

ARC/Architectural Resources Cambridge, Inc.

5 Cambridge Center
Cambridge, MA 02142
617.547.2200
617.547.7222 (Fax)
www.arcusa.com

ARC/Architectural Resources Cambridge, Inc.

St. Paul's School
Athletic and Fitness Center
Concord, New Hampshire

Sports have enriched prestigious St. Paul's School since its founding in 1856 in Concord, New Hampshire, as a boys school that became co-educational in 1971. The birthplace of U.S. ice hockey, St. Paul's began playing the sport in the 1870s. In another first, St. Paul's built America's first squash courts in 1883. So it's fitting that the School recently completed a 150,000-square foot renovation and addition to the existing cage and tennis buildings, designed by ARC/Architectural Resources Cambridge, culminating in the opening of the two-story, 95,000-square foot Athletic and Fitness Center. The Center does more than provide some 535 students with a 460-seat varsity gym, 175-seat junior varsity gym, eight-lane swimming pool, fitness and training facilities, wrestling room, locker rooms and multi-purpose room for aerobics. Thanks to a centrally located, two-story Central Court, it also enables old and new structures to blend successfully with the 2,000-acre campus. Bishop Craig Anderson, former St. Paul's rector, declared, "It's an inspiration to see this building."

Above: Front Facade.
Left: Eight-lane pool.
Bottom left: Fitness room.
Opposite: Central Court.
Photography: Warren Patterson.

10

ARC/Architectural Resources Cambridge, Inc.

Boston College
Yawkey Athletics Center
Chestnut Hill, MA

A distinguished co-educational Jesuit Catholic university founded in 1863, Boston College takes pride in its academic rigor, which benefits its student-athletes as well as the balance of 14,500 undergraduate and graduate students. This all-encompassing commitment to academic excellence has consistently ranked Boston College among the nation's top five colleges and universities in graduation rates of student-athletes. It's one more reason why the new, Yawkey Athletics Center, designed by ARC/Architectural Resources Cambridge, has been erected on the 116-acre Chestnut Hill campus. The Yawkey Athletics Center, a four story, 72,000-square foot new building attached to the north end zone of Alumni Stadium, houses all support spaces for Boston's football team, including a Hall of Fame at the main entry, locker rooms, a 6,000-square foot weight room, training area, 48-seat and 125-seat tiered classrooms, nine breakout rooms, recruiting suite and offices/meeting rooms for coaches, 200-seat, 4,000-square foot function room for recruiting, dining and presentation, and Learning Resource Center. Not only does the Center provide much-needed facilities for football, but it also gives the Office of Learning Resources more space and equipment to help student-athletes maintain their academic achievement. Anticipating the building's impact, Tom O'Brien, Boston's head coach, predicted, "It will be a showcase for Boston College football."

Top: Therapy pools.

Above: Exterior.

Upper right: Tiered classroom..

Right: Hall of Fame.

Opposite top: Locker room.

Opposite bottom left: Weight room.

Opposite bottom right: Alumni Stadium designed by ARC in 1994.

Photography: Warren Patterson.

ARC/Architectural Resources Cambridge, Inc.

University of Massachusetts, Lowell
Campus Recreation Center
Lowell, Massachusetts

Left: Fitness center.

Opposite: Café/Juice Bar.

Below: Exterior at dusk.

Bottom: Control desk in lobby with gymnasium below.

Photography: Warren Patterson.

Practicality and idealism coincide readily on the 125-acre campus of University of Massachusetts, Lowell, an institution founded in 1894 that currently serves over 12,000 resident and commuter students in the historic industrial city of Lowell. The development of fitness and recreation facilities for non-athlete students provides a good example. The new, two-story, 72,550-square foot Campus Recreation Center, designed by ARC/Architectural Resources Cambridge, offers an attractive environment for students to congregate, exercise and play sports, while simultaneously giving residents, commuters and the public a welcoming yet secure place to meet. Most facilities, including a three-court gymnasium, three-lane suspended running track, multi-level fitness center, multi-purpose rooms for aerobics, dance and karate, are restricted to students. However, the building occupies a transitional zone between the University and the community. So, without relinquishing control over non-public areas, the building openly welcomes the public to its popular café/juice bar as sought by the State of Massachusetts. To quote Brad Navis, UMass Lowell's recreational sports director, "It's a real quality of life upgrade for everyone involved."

ARC/Architectural Resources Cambridge, Inc.

Noble & Greenough School
Morrison Athletic Center
Dedham, Massachusetts

Top: Track above gymnasium.
Above: Squash Courts.
Left: New main entry.
Below left: Fitness Center.
Photography: Nick Wheeler.

Originally built in 1936 to accommodate 200 boys, the existing athletic facilities at Noble & Greenough School in Dedham, Massachusetts, were clearly failing the task of supporting the 500 boys and girls on to day's 187-acre campus. ARC first started working with "Nobles" on an Athletic Feasibility Study – which soon lead to the firm's design of a 60,000-square foot addition to the old 35,000 SF gym and fitness center. The new Morrison Athletic Center (MAC) now houses such needed facilities as a 500-seat, two-court gymnasium, six international squash courts, wrestling and aerobics rooms, 3,000-square foot fitness center with attached training room, suspended jogging track, student lounge and new lobby in an open environment where students and visitors can follow activities going on throughout the interiors. Yet the building, like much else at Nobles, a school founded in 1866, keeps up with the times in other ways as well. Besides connecting the campus with the adjacent Charles River, it now acts as a popular focus for campus tours by prospective students and their families. For Robert Henderson, head of Nobles, "The 'MAC' is now one of the hubs of campus life."

Barker Rinker Seacat Architecture, P.C.

2300 Fifteenth Street
Suite 100
Denver, CO 80202
303.455.1366
303.455.7457 (Fax)
www.brsarch.com

Barker Rinker Seacat Architecture, P.C.

Barker Rinker Seacat Architecture

Paul Derda Recreation Center
City and County of Broomfield
Broomfield, Colorado

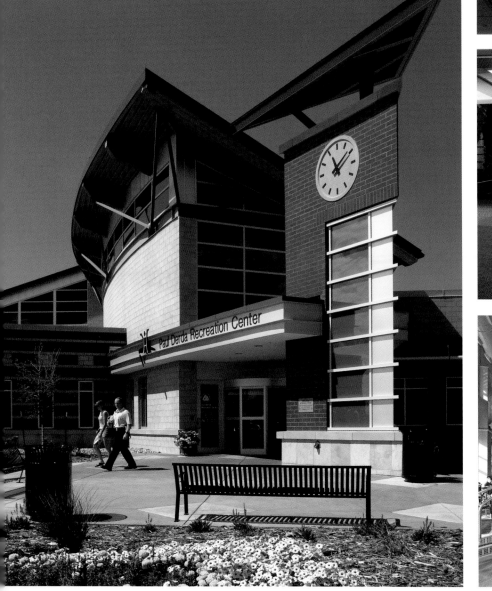

Clockwise from upper left: Exterior, lounge, natatorium, rotunda ceiling skylight.

Photography: Michael Shopenn.

Rocky Mountain vistas are so prized in Colorado that preserving them is often a legal obligation. Still, residents of Broomfield, a Denver suburb of 42,169 residents experience a distinct "wow" upon entering the new, two-story, 84,870-square foot Paul Derda Recreation Center, designed by Barker Rinker Seacat Architecture, in association with Water Technology, Inc. that anchors 338-acre Broomfield Commons. This dynamic, award-winning facility, thoughtfully recessed from the street and tucked into the site's hilly topography to reduce its scale to a nearby residential neighborhood, admits patrons at the upper level, letting them peer down into the extensive activity spaces below—dominated by a spectacular, 12,000-square foot natatorium. Even so, the natatorium is only one of many functions, which include a gymnasium, gymnastics center, aerobics studio, indoor playground, cardiovascular fitness, climbing wall, child care, teen center, yoga studio, party room, lounge, locker rooms, galleria/lobby and administrative offices. Bob Prince, Broomfield's former Director of Recreation, happily observes, "The warmth of the building and its bright colors encourage visitors to come in and have fun."

Above: Walking / jogging track and gymnastics center.

Left: Game room.

Far left: Babysitting/ tot watch room.

**Barker Rinker Seacat Architecture
and Neumann Smith & Associates**

Livonia Community Recreation Center
Livonia, Michigan

Though the City of Livonia intended to convert 56-year-old Bentley High School into a community recreation center, the design team of Barker Rinker Seacat Architecture, Neumann/Smith & Associates and Water Technology, Inc. convinced this Detroit suburb of 100,000 residents that the budget would be smartly spent on new construction. The new, two-level, 130,224-square foot Livonia Recreation Center not only validates the decision through more useable space, improved control and security, reduced staff requirements, life-cycle cost savings and shorter construction time, it introduces an irresistible "mall of fun." Inside its masonry walls and iconic glass cylinder, three blocks of space enclose a commons offering views of the fitness center, rock climbing wall, gymnastics center, gymnasia, adult/senior lounge, daycare center, soft indoor playground and concession area. The glass cylinder justifies its image as well. When visitors at the entry plaza see the aquatic center, they focus on the cylinder's 250-foot-long water flume before noticing the leisure pool, vortex pools, eight-lane, "stretch 25-meter" competition pool, and "lazy river" for water aerobics. Expecting to attract 4,000 to 5,000 memberships, city officials sold 15,000 within six months. "We've been well received," admits Ron Reinke, former Superintendent of the Parks & Recreation Department.

Top right: Exterior.

Above left: "Mall of Fun"/Commons.

Above: Rock climbing wall.

Right: Leisure pool.

Photography: Justin Maconochie.

Barker Rinker Seacat Architecture and Braun & Steidl Architects

The Natatorium Community Recreation and Wellness Center
City of Cuyahoga Falls
Cuyahoga Falls, Ohio

Above: Exterior.

Right: Fitness center.

Far right: Natatorium.

Opposite: Entry gallery and rotunda.

Photography: Dan Cunningham.

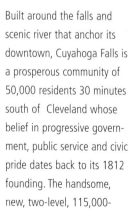

Built around the falls and scenic river that anchor its downtown, Cuyahoga Falls is a prosperous community of 50,000 residents 30 minutes south of Cleveland whose belief in progressive government, public service and civic pride dates back to its 1812 founding. The handsome, new, two-level, 115,000- square foot Community Recreation Center features an Aquatic Center or Natatorium exemplifies this tradition as the replacement for a popular but aging indoor swimming pool that opened in 1965. Designed for the entire family by Barker Rinker Seacat Architecture in association with Braun and Steidl Architects and Water Technology, Inc. the award-winning Center offers a leisure aquatic pool with indoor tube slide, six-lane, 25-yard competition pool, 18-seat hot water spa, and warm water therapy and instructional pool, along with two gymnasiums, group fit- ness rooms, child care, community rooms, racquetball courts and café. Visitors strolling along the soaring entry gallery and rotunda encounter an abundance of ways to play, stay fit and learn wellness in an enlightened city that also hosts the Blossom Music Center, the summer home of the Cleveland Orchestra, and Porthouse Theatre. In assessing the Center, Richard Pierson, former Superintendent, Cuyahoga Falls Parks & Recreation Department, praises its "thorough and unique blending of vision and authenticity."

Barker Rinker Seacat Architecture

Above: Entrance.

Right: Exterior.

Below right: Leisure pool.

Bottom right: Competition pool.

Photography: Jim Barnett (exterior), Jeffrey Totaro (Interior)

Open space is scarce in West Deptford Township, a community of 19,368 residents (2000 census) in Gloucester County, New Jersey, so the transformation of 1,100 acres of Delaware River dredge spoils as the site of the RiverWinds Community Center has brought many welcome changes. Riverfront redevelopment projects have produced sports facilities, senior housing, walking trails, fishing piers, and boat launches in addition to the Center. However, the two-level, 106,483-square foot Center, designed by Barker Rinker Seacat Architecture in association with Wallace Roberts & Todd, is clearly the focal point. Organized around a central control lobby that separates community wing from controlled activity wing, the Center features a 23,600-square foot aquatic center, indoor track, two gymnasiums, wrestling gym, senior center, rock climbing wall, fitness and training area, daycare and outdoor amphitheater. In a recent address, David Shields, former West Deptford mayor, predicted, "This Center is going to help a lot of people, and it feels good."

Cannon Design

Albany
Baltimore
Boston
Buffalo
Chicago
Jacksonville
Los Angeles
New York
San Francisco
St Louis
Toronto
Vancouver
Victoria
Washington, DC

www.cannondesign.com

Cannon Design

University of South Carolina
Strom Thurmond Wellness & Fitness Center
Columbia, South Carolina

A cluster of derelict manufacturing buildings at a busy intersection in Columbia, the state capital of South Carolina, recently vanished—to make room for the University of South Carolina's new Strom Thurmond Wellness & Fitness Center. This two-story, 192,000-square foot facility, designed by Cannon Design with The Boudreaux Group, serves as an icon to both the school and the city. As travelers approch the city at night, this well-lit facility is one of the first landmarks they see. The design reflects the historic character of the 358-acre campus in such contemporary ways as a monumental entry rotunda set beneath a massive, domed skylight, and a sky-lighted, multi-story gallery, functioning as the main circulation spine. The building provides modern physical fitness facilities for a 204-year-old institution serving over 37,800 students. Among the many features are a 1/7-mile running track, natatorium, multi-court gymnasium, 52-foot rock climbing wall, wellness center, multi-purpose aerobics and martial arts rooms, whirlpools, saunas, locker rooms, offices and a café.

Above left: Squash courts and gallery.

Above right: Exterior.

Left: Cardiovascular deck overlooking strength and conditioning room.

Opposite: Natatorium.

Photography: Creative Sources Photography.

Cannon Design

Boston University
Fitness and Recreation Center and Agganis Arena
Boston, Massachusetts

By joining the east and west ends of Boston University's 132-acre campus with 10 acres of new athletic and entertainment facilities plus high-rise housing for 2,300 students, John Hancock Student Village heralds an exciting era in the school's 166-year history. For the first time, a central gathering place exists for BU's 30,000 students and its faculty, alumni and other visitors. The 280,000-square foot Fitness and Recreation Center and 6,200-seat, Agganis Arena play especially critical roles. Designed by Cannon Design, creator of the Student Village concept, the village is a hub of activity with residential, recreation and sports components to create an exciting synergy of activities for the campus community. The Fitness and Recreation Center houses such facilities as a 25-meter competition/lap pool, recreational pool, racquetball and squash courts, dance studio, three- and four-court gymnasiums, jogging track, wellness center and rock climbing wall. The Arena, named for a popular BU athlete and player for the Boston Red Sox, can expand to 7,200 seats for concerts, conventions, trade shows and family entertainment whenever it is not supporting BU's outstanding hockey and basketball programs. It boasts such amenities as private boxes, chairback seating, a well-appointed lounge and two levels of underground parking. School spirit thrives in the Student Village, and BU has much to cheer about.

Top: Aerial.

Above: Exterior.

Below left: Team workout room with running track.

Below bottom: Ice Rink.

Opposite: Fitness center.

Photography: Jon Miller/Hedrich Blessing, Desroches Photography.

Cannon Design

Texas Christian University
Student Recreation Center
Fort Worth, Texas

What do students at Texas Christian University think of their new Recreation Center? With over 8,000 undergraduates and graduate students on the 260-acre Fort Worth campus needing more space for athletic activities, the school recently developed the 224,000-square foot facility by renovating Rickel Hall, a 120,000-square foot, windowless, pre-cast concrete 1970s building, and expanding it with 104,000 square feet of new construction. Judging from the crowds that show up 24/7, the dramatic transformation, designed by Cannon

Design is just what TCU needed. The existing two-court gymnasium has become a volleyball venue and recreation space, and the existing natatorium now includes a 25-yard, six-lane pool with diving well. New construction has added an atrium lobby, three-court gymnasium, 12,000-square foot weight and fitness center, climbing wall, racquetball and squash courts, multi-purpose room and mezzanine-level running track, all enclosed by cream-colored brick that repeats the existing cladding—plus a curving metal roof over the weight and fitness center

to differentiate the award-winning building from its surroundings. By day, extensive glazing floods the Center with sunshine. By night, indoor lighting turns it into a beacon whose friendly glow spreads across the campus.

Above: Exterior.

Upper left: Atrium lobby.

Left: Weight and fitness center.

Opposite: Indoor running track.

Photography: Hedrich Blessing- Jon Miller.

Cannon Design

Crunch Fitness, Lincoln Park
Chicago, Illinois

Above left: Entry.

Above right: Mutli purpose studio as viewed from lobby.

Right: Lobby.

Photography: Hedrich Blessing.

Described as "part gym, part nightclub," the new, 46,000-square foot Crunch Fitness designed by Cannon Design, is probably all that and more to residents of Chicago's upscale Lincoln Park neighborhood. This recent addition to the 16-year-old chain of some two dozen Crunch Fitness gyms serving nearly 100,000 members across the nation occupies levels three, four and five of a new, mixed-use development. The design uses dynamic architectural elements at every level to draw patrons and prospective members throughout the space. Needless to say, the facility consistently delivers.

Crunch Fitness, may well be the Windy City's finest fitness and wellness facility, featuring backlit juice bar, angular stair and fiber-optic, edge-lit glass wall at the entrance to the general workout areas, swimming pool, multi-purpose studios, rehabilitation clinic, boxing ring, children's room, retail sales area and locker room. The club also features a fifth floor sun deck that provides outstanding views of the Chicago skyline.

Dattner Architects

130 W 57th Street
Suite 3C
New York, NY 10019
212.247.2660
212.245.7132 (Fax)
www.dattner.com

Dattner Architects

Above: Spectator entrance.

Above right: 50-meter pool under curved roof.

Far left: Pool-level entrance.

Left: Diving well and 10-meter tower.

Photography: Peter Mauss/Esto

When the Goodwill Games, an international athletic competition originated by media mogul Ted Turner in 1985, chose New York for the 1998 Games, Dattner Architects, the designer of the 82,000-square foot facility that would host the aquatic events in suburban East Meadow, faced two formidable challenges. First, the Goodwill Games Swimming and Diving Complex would have to fit unobtrusively into the natural landscape of the site, Eisenhower Park. Second, the Complex would have to totally support a world-class event, as promised to the Games by New York State's organizers, before converting into a year-round community recreation facility. The first challenge was met by lowering the building partly below grade and enclosing it with a curved roof. The second one was resolved with a south façade that could be raised to provide 1,600 temporary seats during the Games to supplement 3,000 permanent ones. As attendees of the Games and visitors to Eisenhower Park will happily attest, the 50-meter by 25-meter pool with movable bulkheads, diving well and 10-meter tower have performed superbly.

Dattner Architects

University of Pennsylvania
Pottruck Health and Fitness Center
Philadelphia, Pennsylvania

Left: Exterior.

Below left: Through-floor views.

Opposite: Atrium.

Photography: Kevin Chut + Jessica Paul

Benjamin Franklin, the pragmatic and inquisitive statesman who founded the University of Pennsylvania in 1751, would have promptly seen the wisdom of introducing the handsome, new Pottruck Health and Fitness Center, designed by Dattner Architects, to campus life. The Center acts as the keystone in the development of the University's state-of-the-art, 120,000-square foot recreation and wellness complex by combining 70,000 square feet of new facilities—including a climbing wall, multi-purpose rooms for dance, martial arts and aerobic activities, a golf simulator, spinning room, locker rooms, pro shop and juice bar—with 50,000 square feet of existing and upgraded ones in the adjacent Gimbel Gymnasium and Sheer Pool. The resulting complex is unified by creating a sky-lit atrium, creating a new campus walk whose cascading stairs and bridges link the two structures while maintaining their separate identities. With today's recreational activities expanding well beyond the simple push-ups, chin-ups and weight lifting that satisfied earlier generations of students, it's easy to imagine the University's famous founder trying something new at the Center.

Dattner Architects

Asphalt Green AquaCenter
New York, New York

Miracles happen even in modern America, as New York's Asphalt Green demonstrates. This not-for-profit sports and fitness organization, occupying a 5-1/2-acre campus in Manhattan's Upper East Side, was created by private citizens who transformed a desolate urban lot into a resource for children and families. Named for the parabolic-shaped Municipal Asphalt Plant constructed in 1944 and converted to a sports center in 1982, the "Green" became so popular that it has added an attractive, five-story, 75,000-square foot AquaCenter, designed by Dattner Architects. The AquaCenter is larger than its tight urban site, wedged between a playground, a truck ramp and a highway bordering the Hudson River, would suggest. Besides the modern, 50-meter, eight-lane Olympic-sized pool forming its base, equipped with competition gutters, recirculation systems, movable bulkheads, hydraulic, movable floor and seating for 700, fitness facilities and administrative offices fill the upper floors. If the Aqua- Center isn't a miracle, it comes close.

Top: Aerial view.

Above: Exterior.

Above left: Entrance to AquaCenter.

Opposite: 50-meter pool and 700-seat gallery.

Photographer: Jeff Goldberg/ESTO

Dattner Architects

Hudson River Park
Pier 96 Boathouse
New York, New York

Less is truly more at the new, 6,700-square foot Pier 96 Boathouse, designed by Dattner Architects for the Hudson River Park Trust with minimal detailing as one of three boathouses planned for Piers 66, 84 and 96 at New York City's Hudson River Park. A floating pier for boat launching, which rises and falls with the tide, provides boaters and their non-motorized craft with unencumbered access to the water via a wide bridge leading from the river side of the boathouse. In addition, the construction of the boathouse emphasizes environmentally-conscious, energy-efficient design, minimizing maintenance, mechanical requirements and energy consumption through such means as recyclable, low embedded-energy materials like cement board siding and zinc roofing, large sliding doors that promote cross ventilation, translucent clerestory panels installed to give abundant lighting, and ridge vents that provide natural convection. Even the locations of the boathouses have been coordinated with U.S. Army Corps of Engineers guidelines to improve life for breeding fish as well as boating New Yorkers, making the boathouses appropriate signposts for Hudson River Park, one of New York's most ambitious public projects, encompassing over 550 acres of parkland along the water's edge from Manhattan's southern tip to West 59th Street.

Top: Pier 96 Boathouse and floating pier.

Upper left: Interior.

Lower left: Twilight view.

Photography: Ruggero Vanni.

David M. Schwarz/Architectural Services, Inc.

1707 L Street N. W.
Suite 400
Washington, D.C. 20036
202.862.0777
202.331.0507 (Fax)
www.dmsas.com

David M. Schwarz/Architectural Services, Inc.

David M. Schwarz/Architectural Services, Inc.

Dr Pepper / 7•Up Ballpark
Frisco, Texas

Even before the first pitch at Dr Pepper/7-Up Ballpark, residents of Frisco, Texas could see that the new home of the Frisco RoughRiders, a Double-A affiliate of the Texas Rangers, was unlike other stadiums. The charming, 10,500-seat, 230,000-square foot facility, designed with a coastal Galveston aesthetic by David M. Schwarz/ Architectural Services, represented a "baseball park within a park," a landscaped, 65-acre mixed-use site. To meet tight budgets and schedule, the seating bowl was built on grade going down 14 feet from the concourse level, and four independent, two- and four-story pavilions, clad in gray clapboard siding with white trim, were constructed along the back of the seating bowl to house concessions and restrooms on the concourse level. On the upper level, these pavilions house 29 luxury suites seating 350 patrons. However, there's no sense of expediency in this product of a private-public partnership. In fact, the public adores this award-winning, village-like ballpark.

Top: Ticketing area.

Above: Home plate entrance.

Left: Seating bowl and pavilions.

Opposite: Outdoor bridges connecting pavilions.

Photography: Steve Hall/ Hedrich/Blessing Photographers.

David M. Schwarz/Architectural Services, Inc. Ameriquest Field/The Ballpark in Arlington
Arlington, Texas

"We want everyone across the country to recognize this as Texas." To fulfill this goal, the Texas Rangers built award-winning Ameriquest Field in Arlington, a 49,000-seat open-air ballpark designed by David M. Schwarz/Architectural Services, that opened to public acclaim in 1994. The majestic, brick-and-granite structure is the centerpiece of a 270-acre community center, master planned by DMS/AS, that also accommodates a youth ballpark, amphitheater, learning center, sports hall of fame and riverwalk with festival retailing. Traditional in appearance to evoke baseball's history and Texas' heritage, Ameriquest Field is uncompromisingly modern in con-

struction, operations and amenities. Its five levels of seating, featuring club seating and 120 suites, are arrayed on four levels-service level, main concourse, club concourse and upper concourse, forming a seating bowl that nests within the exterior walls and encloses grand concourse spaces, interior pedestrian ramps and refuge from the region's frequent summer thunderstorms. Does Ameriquest Field represent Texas? You bet.

Above left: Seating bowl.

Above right: Outer main concourse.

Right: Aerial view.

Opposite: Homeplate Gate.

Photography: Jim Hedrich/Hedrich Blessing, SkyCam.

David M. Schwarz/Architectural Services, Inc.   American Airlines Center
Dallas, Texas

Not quite five years old, American Airlines Center, an award-winning, 20,000-seat, 840,000-square foot arena designed by David M. Schwarz/Architectural Services with HKS to house the NBA's Dallas Mavericks and the NHL's Dallas Stars, is already a Dallas landmark. Credit its striking architecture of brick, limestone and granite walls topped by a roof bearing four signature arches, and its highly visible location on 75-acre site Victory Park, a lively, pedestrian-friendly, mixed-use development being created from former industrial land. The 150,000-square-foot, double-barrel vaulted roof not only creates a distinctive profile spanning all four facades; it optimizes the number of structural members required. Employing a unique, retractable seating system to accelerate conversions between basketball and hockey, the seating bowl is encircled by four perimeter lobbies at the main concourse level whose location, high degree of finish, (including terrazzo floors, windows and crown molding), and individual themes and concessions let visitors enjoy knowing exactly where they are.

Top: Exterior and downtown.

Above left: Main concourse.

Above right: Arena in hockey configuration.

Right: Lobby stair.

Opposite: Perimeter lobby.

Photography: Steve Hall/ Hedrich Blessing.

David M. Schwarz/Architectural Services, Inc.

Disney's Wide World of Sports, Walt Disney World Resort
Lake Buena Vista, Florida

Left: Interior of Milk House.

Above: Seating bowl of Cracker Jack ® Stadium.

Bottom left: Milk House's main entrance.

Photography: Dan Forer

Are the traditions of small-town planning versatile enough to produce a 240-acre, international sports complex in central Florida that is not only a great venue for sports playing and viewing, but also a charming and comfortable place where people can stroll, get out of the sun, sip a cool drink, and return again and again? Take a walk through the lush landscape and "Florida Picturesque" architecture of Disney's Wide World of Sports at Walt Disney World Resort in Orlando. Here, David M. Schwarz/ Architectural Services has provided master planning and worked with HKS to design two key facilities, the 9,500-seat, Cracker Jack ® Stadium, a Triple-A ballpark and spring training facility for the Atlanta Braves, and the 34,000-square-foot Milk House, a field house capable of housing over 25 AAU championship competitions as well as other amateur events. With town square and town green as focal points, the stadium and field house establish their own identities while enriching the surrounding blend of Mediterranean, Spanish, Venetian Gothic and Southern California styles, introducing something new yet timeless under the Florida sun.

ELS
Architecture and Urban Design

2040 Addison Street
Berkeley, CA 94704
510.549.2929
510.843.3304 (Fax)
www.elsarch.com
info@elsarch.com

Stanford University
Avery Aquatic Center
Stanford, California

One of America's finest outdoor aquatic facilities, Stanford University's deGuerre Pool Complex has re-emerged bigger and better as the award-winning, 77,360-square foot Avery Aquatic Center, designed by ELS. Two new world-class pools, the Belardy 50-meter training pool and Maas Family Diving Complex, give the Cardinal teams for swimming, diving, water polo and synchronized swimming a superior home for Olympic-level training that aids campus recreation and attracts national and international competitions. The Maas Diving Complex— a campus landmark—introduces a diving tower with five platforms plus four springboards, dive tank, and warm-up spa. ELS has refurbished the competition pool for water polo so major events in all four aquatic sports can be hosted, supported by new locker rooms, offices, shade canopy for 2400, and other accommodations that were added. New night lighting keeps everyone "in the swim" even after dark. Richard Quick, Stanford's women's swimming coach, describes Avery as "the finest training and competition aquatic facilities in the world."

Top: Aerial view of center.

Above: Canopy over pool seating.

Right: Close up of dive tower.

Opposite: 10 meter tower.

Photography: David Wakely, Steve Proehl (top).

To promote Morgan Hill's values of health, fitness and environment, this growing community located at the southern end of California's famed Silicon Valley, has developed the family-friendly Morgan Hill Aquatic Center. The award-winning competition and recreational swimming facility, designed by ELS, stands out as both a bustling athletic and social gathering place and an effective, environmentally responsive design. Its ambitious program is supported by a 50-meter competition pool, 6,000-square foot activity pool with play structures and waterslide, 6-lane lap/instructional pool, and a "sprayground." The pools and the 8,825-square foot pool house, mechanical building and group picnic areas sit on 8.5 acres. The crisply delineated, contemporary design is largely driven by two key concepts: an efficient layout that separates competition and recreation events occuring simultaneously, and a comprehensive approach to sustainability with recycled and low maintenance materials, low-energy consumption, wind protection and efficient water use—California's first LEED Silver-rated aquatic facility. "This is another gem for this community," proclaims Morgan Hill mayor Dennis Kennedy. "It is everything we hoped for and more."

Top: Arrival plaza.

Middle: Competition pool with windscreen.

Bottom: Sportsfield and foothills beyond.

Opposite: Poolside entry.

Photography: David Wakely.

ELS

Berkeley High School, the only public high school serving Berkeley, California, has enhanced an already proud record of academic excellence, architectural distinction and community involvement with the completion of the new 86,000 square foot Student Union and Recreation Center for its 3000 students. The two-building complex, designed by ELS, comprises a competition pool, gymnasium, student union and dining hall, library, administrative offices and college counseling center. It increases vitality on campus and encourages community after-hours use by providing a light filled, open environment where spaces flow into one another. To minimize corridors, program activities and recreational facilities are near the student union and the dining hall. Counseling offices open to the student dining area, encouraging office visits. The student union is connected to the gymnasium through a glassed-in breezeway. The sliding glass walls that open between the two rooms create a sizeable space large enough to hold community and school-wide events. The breezeway entrance aligns with the city street grid, leading downtown and to public transit. Mindful of its neighbors in Berkeley's landmark Civic Center Historic District,

Above: Gym.

Left: Upper level dance studio.

Opposite above: New gym entrance facing historic campus quad.

Opposite below: Gym overlook.

Photography: David Wakely, Tim Hursley (above right).

ELS

including three Art Deco campus structures, the new buildings blend in gracefully through modern elevations modeled in board-form concrete, steel panels in off-white and soft gray, and large expanses of glass. The complex is bright and comfortable year-round, exceeding California energy standards by 35 percent. Popular and heavily used, the buildings support the social interaction essential to the school's educational mission, create a new central quad envisioned in the 1930s master plan, and reconnect the high school to its urban community.

Top: Natatorium exterior.

Middle: Natatorium with swimmers starting. Open to campus views.

Bottom: View of campus quad from pool.

Photography: Tim Hursley (top), David Wakely (middle), ELS (bottom).

EwingCole

Federal Reserve Bank Building
100 North 6th Street
Philadelphia, PA 19106
215.923.2020
215.351.5346 (Fax)
www.ewingcole.com

EwingCole

Monmouth University
Multi-Use Activity Center
West Long Branch, New Jersey

Encouraging evidence of how architecture is supporting the wave of athletic diversification now enlisting young and old alike can be observed at Monmouth University. Here a new, 160,000-square foot Multi-Use Activity Center, designed by EwingCole, is nearing completion. The "MAC," a freestanding addition to an existing athletic facility, will offer students and faculty enhanced recreational options and a venue for NCAA Division I competition. It introduces a 5,500-seat arena/gymnasium, indoor track, fitness area, varsity training area, hall of fame, premium suites, locker rooms, administrative offices, college bookstore/copy center and academic learning center.

Despite the building's massive scale, its impact on the surrounding residential neighborhood will be benign, by siting the new building in the heart of campus and thanks to an outreach program conducted by Monmouth and EwingCole that addressed residents' concerns. Consequently, the MAC will take its place in a new campus center that

should enrich life for some 6,000 students on Monmouth's 153 acres, attract prospective students, and improve town-gown relations as well.

Above: Exterior.

Left: Arena.

Lower right: Weight and fitness.

Bottom right: Corridor.

Illustrations: Courtesy of EwingCole, Digital rendering by AEI Digital.

EwingCole

Duncaster Wellness Center
Bloomfield, Connecticut

"Active seniors" is not a 21st century oxymoron, judging from the interest among today's elderly in the athletic lifestyle. Even among continuing care facilities, recreational centers are opening where a holistic approach to living promotes fitness and wellness. Such a facility is the new, 12,000-square foot Wellness Center at Duncaster, a continuing care adult community in Bloomfield, Connecticut. The challenge for EwingCole, designer of the freestanding addition to Duncaster's 87-acre grounds, has been to create a destination where residents feel welcome and active, yet anticipate the decreased mobility of many individuals. The Center's facilities, including a natatorium, fitness facilities, locker rooms, lounges and café, shrewdly emulate top-notch health and fitness clubs. Not only do they provide such desirable features as a zero-entry swimming pool with views of the exterior courtyard, they are appointed in classic furnishings that reflect the inviting, home-like décor of Duncaster's residential areas. Don't "active seniors" enjoy comfort too?

Top: Natatorium.
Left: Exterior.
Above: Natatorium.
Opposite: Entry lobby.
Photography: Jeffrey Totaro.

EwingCole

Bucknell University
Kenneth G. Langone Athletic & Recreation Center
Lewisburg, Pennsylvania

A respected liberal arts college founded in 1846, Bucknell University uses sports and recreation to enhance the quality of life for 3,400 undergraduates and 150 graduate students on its 450-acre campus in Lewisburg, Pennsylvania. Consider the new, 180,000-square foot Kenneth G. Langone Athletic & Recreation Center. It was designed by EwingCole as a free-standing addition to the Gerhard Fieldhouse and historic Davis Gymnasium. Visitors readily appreciate the Center's extensive offerings because its open, airy and appealing environment provides deliberate views to adjacent program areas wherever they may be. There are three major venues, the 4,000-seat Sojka Pavilion for basketball, the 500-seat, 50-meter x 25-yard Kinney Natatorium for swimming, diving and water polo, and the Krebs Family Fitness Center for weights and exercise. Additionally, numerous other athletic facilities, lounges and a café offer a wealth of activities to see and do for students, faculty, staff, alumni, and varsity student-athletes.

Top: Campus vista.

Left: Dusk arrival.

Bottom left: Cardio mezzanine.

Bottom right: Multi-level fitness center.

Opposite: Entry lobby & Hall of Fame.

Photographer: Jeffrey Totaro.

For every college or university varsity athlete there are countless other students who simply enjoy sports and recreation. The two increasingly require facilities that serve a diversity of activities, a goal EwingCole has achieved by designing the Kenneth G. Langone Athletic & Recreation Center and partially remodeling existing athletic buildings. Combining varsity training and general student recreation under one roof is challenging. The design seeks ways to make all visitors comfortable. Bucknell's athletic facilities enhance its 26 varsity athletics programs and expand the scope of its intramural sports and recreation through careful space planning that concentrates related activities in dedicated areas. In the Langone Center, for example, easy wayfinding through the gymnasium, arena, natatorium, student fitness, varsity training, hall of fame, locker rooms and administrative offices tells students what's available and where to go.

Top right: Sojka pavilion.
Right: Instructional weights.
Below right: Fitness center stair.
Below: Kinney Natatorium.
Opposite: Exterior.
Photographer: Jeffrey Totaro.

EwingCole

Citizens Bank Park
Philadelphia, Pennsylvania

One of the most spectacular ways modern ballparks excel, as demonstrated by the new home of Major League Baseball's Philadelphia Phillies, the 43,500-seat, 1.15-million square foot Citizens Bank Park, designed by EwingCole, is that they serve fans as well as athletes. Citizens Bank Park enhances the spectator's experience by creating attractive opportunities for socializing and entertainment before and during the game. The experi- ence begins as fans arrive at the 21-acre site where I-76, I-95 and the southern termi- nus of the Broad Street Subway converge, and are welcomed into the contem- porary ballpark through landscaped entry plazas at the four corners of the site. Inside, the action revolves around good seating with unobstructed sight lines overlooking the game and views of Center City, as well as conveniently located and inviting ticket offices, restau- rants, retail shops and offices. A day at Citizens Bank Park is like old time baseball—only better.

Above left: View of the out- field and city skyline.

Left: Entrance plaza.

Opposite: Outfield & Ashburn Alley.

Photography: Jeffrey Totaro.

Ballpark outings have always been about the game. Nevertheless, EwingCole's design of Citizens Bank Park shows how sports venues now draw inspiration from the hospitality and entertainment worlds to give patrons memorable experiences. First, the ballpark's distinctive modern architecture of brick and steel establishes a dramatic setting for any event. While purchasers of premium seating can choose luxury suites, club level seats, or lower bowl level Diamond Club seats, an impressive 45 percent of all seating is at field level, and everyone enjoys a clear view of the game. There's also a wide range of dining and entertainment options besides traditional ballpark concessions, such as Harry the K's, a two-level restaurant and bar, Bull's BBQ, an outdoor establishment named for Greg "The Bull" Luzinski, Ashburn Alley, an open-air entertainment plaza, and The Cooperstown Gallery, an interactive display featuring the Phillies' Hall of Fame players. Of course, there's baseball too.

Top right: Diamond club lounge.

Top left: Phillies clubhouse.

Upper left: Suite.

Left: Diamond club.

Lower left: Ashburn Suite.

Opposite: Team store.

Photographer: Jeffrey Totaro.

Boardwalk Hall
Atlantic City, New Jersey

Miss America liked it so much she moved in and stayed from 1940-2005. Today, Atlantic City's 79-year-old, 13,800-seat Boardwalk has never looked more alluring, thanks to an award-winning renovation designed by EwingCole. Modernized acoustics, lighting and other building systems, restored Beaux Arts interiors and a new seating bowl with excellent sight lines are among the far-reaching consequences for the National Historic Landmark. Equally important, Boardwalk Hall is now easier to reconfigure, streamlining its operations and reducing its expenses as a popular showcase for professional boxing matches, Disney on Ice, Ringling Bros. and Barnum & Bailey Circus and such entertainers as Bruce Springsteen, Paul McCartney, Bette Midler and Elton John. To quote Barbara Lampen, vice president of the New Jersey Sport & Exposition Authority, "EwingCole exhibited extraordinary vision and innovative design technique in transforming the historic Atlantic City convention hall into a state-of-the-arts special events center."

Top: Full auditorium view.

Above: Arch with capital detail.

Above left: Historic gallery arcade.

Opposite: Concourse.

Photography: Tom Crane, Jeffrey Totaro.

Sections 111 112
211 212

EwingCole

George Mason University
Athletics & Recreation Master Plan
Fairfax, Virginia

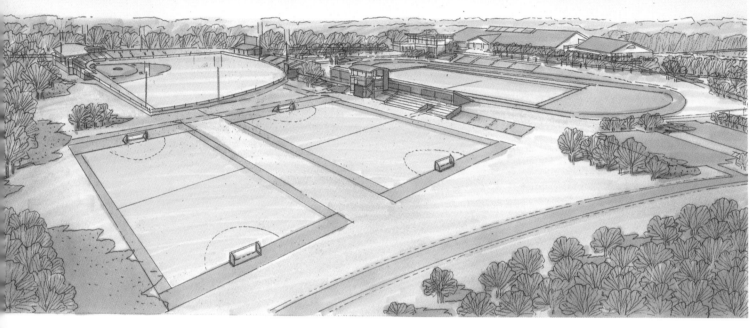

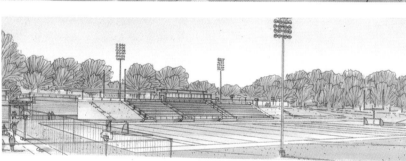

Great college and university campuses are not created haphazardly. Indeed, they are typically the result of advanced planning that exploits architecture's ability to promote spatial connectivity. By preparing a master plan of comprehensive improvements and additions to the sports and recreation facilities for the 557-acre campus of George Mason University in Fairfax, Virginia, EwingCole has created strategies for maximizing the athletic experience for its 22,890 students. These strategies will not only enrich campus life for students, faculty, staff and alumni, they will help to unite the campus through a series of related destinations, support a long-term institutional mission to manage dramatic growth in the next decade, and give prospective students still more compelling reasons to seek admission to George Mason University.

Top: Recreational center.

Center: Aerial view of west campus.

Above left: Basketball training facility.

Above right: Robinson field.

Right: West campus concept plan.

Illustrations: EwingCole.

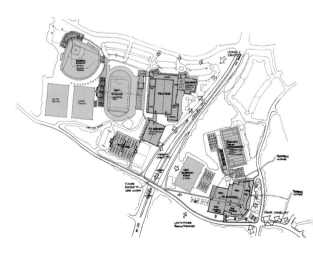

Hastings & Chivetta Architects, Inc.

700 Corporate Park Drive
Suite 400
St. Louis, MO 63105
314.863.5717
314.863.2823 (Fax)
www.hastingschivetta.com

Hastings & Chivetta Architects, Inc.   Riverplex
Peoria, Illinois

"But will it play in Peoria?" is a time-honored question this city of 112,936 residents, Illinois' oldest community, proudly answers with a resounding "yes." A three-time, All-American city that is world headquarters for Caterpillar, Inc., Peoria recently joined forces with OSF Saint Francis Medical Center to build the new, two-level, 125,000-square foot Riverplex, a sports and wellness facility designed by Hastings & Chivetta Architects, that reinforces Peoria's reputation for sophis-ticated yet tradition-minded living by advancing the Peoria Riverfront Business District's master plan. What makes Riverplex particularly interesting is its ability to revitalize Peoria's riverfront and meet the Medical Center's goals with a health and fitness center, indoor water park with four pools, three-court multi-purpose arena, 1/8-mile track, classrooms, including demonstration kitchen, restaurant/food court, child care facilities, and pro shop. Riverplex plays in Peoria—like a champion.

Above left: Arena and exterior.
Above right: Entry lobby.
Opposite: Water park.
Photography: Sam Fentress.

Hastings & Chivetta Architects, Inc.   The Lodge Des Peres
Des Peres, Missouri

Des Peres, Missouri, a suburban St. Louis community inhabited since the 1700s but not incorporated as a village until 1934, has developed into a thriving city of 8,592 residents (2000 Census) by taking a deliberate yet enlightened view of civic responsibilities under the city administrator form of governance. An impressive example of its public works is The Lodge Des Peres, a new, two-level, 76,365-square foot community recreation center, designed by Hastings & Chivetta Architects. The facility deliberately appeals to residents of all ages. Its warm and

inviting "lodge-like" building houses a two-court, multi-purpose gymnasium, elevated jogging track, two-story weight and fitness area, snack bar, wet classroom for aquatics, indoor six-lane pool with zero-depth entry and wave feature, 20-person whirlpool, toddler splash deck, enclosed tube slide that exits and re-enters the building with a 26-foot skim out for small children, locker rooms, shared steam and sauna, and multi-purpose dance and aerobics room, as well as an extensive outdoor water park. Superbly placed and landscaped on a sloping, nearly 11-acre site, it is

planned so parents can see their children anywhere in the water park. Praising the architect for the design of The Lodge, Susan Trautman, director of Parks and Recreation for Des Peres, declares, "This team has set a new standard for community centers."

Above: Exterior and water park.

Upper left: Lobby lounge.

Left: Indoor pool.

Opposite: Entrance lobby.

Photography: Sam Fentress.

76

Hastings & Chivetta Architects, Inc.

The Heights Community Center
Richmond Heights, Missouri

Above: Exterior.
Left: Aquatic center.
Far left: Library.
Opposite: Rotunda.
Photography: Sam Fentress.

Armed with cell phones, laptops and the like, Americans are becoming surprisingly adept at "multi-tasking," so it's easy to see why the residents of Richmond Heights, Missouri would make similar demands on their splendid new public facility, The Heights Community Center. To save space, time and money, the two-story, 73,167-square foot, Neoclassical building, designed by Hastings & Chivetta Architects, gathers open and programmed recreation, team sports, meeting spaces and public library under one roof through careful zoning and acoustic separation. This allows people of all ages to enjoy the diverse activity areas organized around the building's main entry and lobby, housed inside the majestic, two-story rotunda, such as the aquatic center, gymnasium, weight training area, three-lane track, dividable meeting room, catering kitchen, game room, lounge, tot-care facility, locker rooms, 55.000-volume library, storage rooms and office. Teresa Proebsting, director of Parks and Recreation for Richmond Heights, compliments the way "Hastings & Chivetta asked for owner's input, incorporating those ideas into the design."

Hastings & Chivetta Architects, Inc.

Rec-Plex
St. Peters, Missouri

Left: Competition pool.

Above: Ice arena/exhibition area.

Below left: Two-court gym.

Below right: Exterior.

Photography: Sam Fentress.

One of Missouri's fastest growing cities with some 57,000 young, well-educated and prosperous residents, St. Peters uses urban development to advance its progressive agenda. Its new, two-level, 125,000-square foot Rec-Plex, designed by Hastings & Chivetta Architects, gives residents an eye-catching, innovative yet cost-effective venue for sports and recreation, including a 50-meter competition pool with diving well, leisure pool with corkscrew water slide and other features, whirlpool spa, two-court gymnasium, jogging track, rock-climbing wall, aerobic/dance studio, weight training, indoor ice arena/summer exhibition area, food court and game room. A model of efficiency, the Rec-Plex easily handles large crowds with minimal staffing.

Hastings & Chivetta Architects, Inc.

700 Corporate Park Drive
Suite 400
St. Louis, MO 63105
314.863.5717
314.863.2823 (Fax)
www.hastingschivetta.com

Hastings & Chivetta Architects, Inc.

Georgia Institute of Technology
Campus Recreation Center
Atlanta, Georgia

Above: Exterior.

Top right: Competition pool.

Above right: Commons.

Above far right: Café.

Photography: Sam Fentress.

"Wow!" At Georgia Institute of Technology, one of America's top research universities for science and technology, the new, six-level, 298,888-square foot Campus Recreation Center is as impressive as any academic building on its 400-acre Atlanta campus. In fact, the metal-and-glass structure, designed by Hastings & Chivetta Architects to renovate and expand an aging facility built in 1977, consistently gets a "wow" from onlookers. The Center provides modern accommodations for recreation and aquatic sports in a spacious and open environment that attracts growing numbers of Georgia Tech's 16,500 students as well as prospective applicants. Its development began when Georgia Tech was designated as the site of the 1996 Olympic swimming and diving competitions, and a 15,000-seat, freestanding venue with 13,000 temporary seats was attached to the existing structure for the Summer Games. Within the existing building, an intermediate floor was introduced at the fourth level, adding some 60,000 square feet of new space above an existing pool, while other levels were thoroughly renovated—except for the existing roof and its solar panels, part of a 25-year research project being conducted by Georgia Tech, Georgia Power and the U.S. Department of Energy. Final score: a 50-meter competition pool and diving well, leisure pool, six-court gym, auxiliary gym, four racquetball courts, fitness areas, multi-purpose spaces, locker rooms, jogging track, café, offices and support spaces for 8,300 occupants. "Wow" indeed.

Hastings & Chivetta Architects, Inc.

Chatham College
Athletics & Fitness Center
Pittsburgh, Pennsylvania

Chatham College cannot grow beyond its magnificent, 32-acre, park-like campus near the original estate of Andrew Mellon. Here the towering trees, wandering paths and timeless architecture, including century-old mansions transformed into residence halls, have created an idyllic setting near downtown Pittsburgh for the 136-year-old school. To fit Chatham's new 72,023-square foot Athletics & Fitness Building on a narrow, steeply sloping site adjacent to a residential neighborhood, Hastings & Chivetta Architects has wisely chosen to expand vertically rather than horizontally, nestling

four levels of activity areas into the side of the hill. Lowering the natatorium level one floor below grade and stacking the gymnasium above it enables the south façade to assume a residential scale and massing appropriate for the homes it surrounds. The compact footprint of the building is easily navigated along a monumental, three-story stairway that connects the campus grounds with the spectator level two floors, above, so visitors may pass through the building in the "free" zone. Passersby might not realize that what resembles a handsome, Neoclassical residence faced in brick and

stone provides 2,463 occupants with an eight-lane, 25-yard swimming pool with diving well, two-court gymnasium, suspended jogging track, two squash courts, climbing wall, dance studio, fitness center, lockers, offices, classroom and other support spaces. However, the arrangement suits residents of the Squirrel Hill neighborhood perfectly, including Chatham College.

Above: Staircase.

Right: Swimming pool.

Far right: Fitness center.

Opposite above: south façade.

Opposite below: Climbing wall.

Photography: Sam Fentress.

Hastings & Chivetta Architects, Inc.

University of Central Oklahoma
Recreation & Wellness Center
Edmond, Oklahoma

Above: Exterior.

Right: Juice bar.

Far right: Rotunda.

Photography: Sam Fentress.

Do recreation and health services make good campus roommates? Judging from the University of Central Oklahoma's new, 57,140-square foot Recreation & Wellness Center in Edmond, designed by Hastings & Chivetta Architects, the combination serves some 15,500 students quite well. Thus, the Center's two wings, joined by a rotunda, provide a reception/waiting area, examination rooms, laboratories, classrooms and offices for health care, and a two-court gymnasium, lockers, fitness center, running track, juice bar and offices for the recreation departments. In addition, the facility represents both a homage to tradition, reprising the Neoclassical architecture of the 115-year-old University's original signature buildings, and an anticipation of future needs, maintaining a flexible platform for space, power and data. G. Douglas Fox, project coordinator for the University, lauds the Center for being "as close to a perfect building" as possible.

Hastings & Chivetta Architects, Inc.

University of Tulsa
Fulton and Susie Collins Fitness Center
Tulsa, Oklahoma

Making physical fitness an integral part of campus life at the University of Tulsa, a 111-year-old Oklahoma institution affiliated with the Presbyterian Church that serves 4,174 students, has been a long-cherished goal for benefactors Fulton and Susie Collins. Now, with their generous assistance, the University has opened the new, two-level, 67,192-square foot Fulton and Susie Collins Fitness Center, designed by Hastings & Chivetta Architects in the Collegiate Gothic style of architecture that character-izes the campus. It gives students a spacious, colorful and well-lighted gathering place for socializing. For along with a three-court gymnasium, weight and cardiovascular room, multi-purpose aerobics room, wellness center and suspended indoor track, there are such facilities as a lounge, game room and cardio-theater with multi-media TV wall. Expressing her complete satisfaction with the facility, Mary Wafer Johnston, director of campus recreation for the University, happily notes, "Hastings & Chivetta listened to me."

Above: Gymnasium and indoor track.

Left: Exterior.

Lower left: Lounge.

Photography: Sam Fentress.

Hughes Group Architects

45640 Willow Pond Plaza
Sterling, Virginia 20164
703.437.6600
703.834.1752 (Fax)
www.hgaarch.com

Hughes Group Architects

University of Houston
Campus Recreation & Wellness Center
Houston, Texas

"Awesome." That's the word used by the University of Houston's students, to describe their new two-story, 264,000-square foot Campus Recreation & Wellness Center designed by Hughes Group Architects. The cliché gains credibility once you visit the award-winning facility at the main entrance to the campus. Managing to be simultaneously enormous, comprehensive and user-friendly, the popular Center provides social, recreational and wellness services to students, faculty and staff in an environment designed as a miniature city. A spacious, palm-filled atrium acts as a calm, unifying element and congenial crossroads. The 53-foot rock climbing wall is visible from virtually everywhere. Clear views of the campus and Houston skyline keep occupants in contact with the world around them and daylight pours in from every possible angle to create an atmosphere where everyone feels welcome. There's no shortage of activity to sample, such as: five basketball courts, an aerobics room, "MAC" zone for soccer, tennis, roller hockey or team handball, 107 machines for cardiovascular exercise, 32,000 pounds of free-weights, overhead fitness track, racquetball, handball and squash courts, a 70-meter pool and 10-meter diving facility, a 4,800-square foot outdoor pool, outdoor soccer fields, multi-purpose rooms, childcare, wellness suite, locker rooms, and a café and convenience store. How else but awesome would students describe the brick, granite and glass-clad building, one of the newest of a new breed of all-inclusive recreation centers designed to recruit and keep students on campus?

Above: Exterior.

Upper left: Basketball court.

Lower left: Pool and diving facility.

Opposite: Atrium.

Photography: Timothy Hursley.

Hughes Group Architects

George Mason University
Aquatic and Fitness Center
Fairfax, Virginia

Above: Competition pool.
Left: Entry pavilion.
Far Left: Exterior.
Photography: Dan Cunningham.

Even dedicated scholars must take an occasional break. Founded as the Northern Virginia branch of the University of Virginia in 1957, George Mason University has evolved into an independent and internationally recognized institution with 28,874 students on its 677-acre Fairfax campus. However, it lacked a major facility where students, faculty and staff could compete in aquatic events, stay fit or just relax, until the opening of the new two-story, 67,500-square foot Aquatic and Fitness Center designed by Hughes Group Architects. Occupying the southeast corner of the campus ring road, the brick and concrete structure announces its presence through a graceful arched natatorium and luminous entry pavilion which draw eager visitors to such attractive and accessible features as a 50-meter competition pool, 25-yard recreational pool, exercise, aerobic and weight rooms, plus various instructional and administrative support spaces. The campus has definitely noticed—and University officials applaud the "wonderful sense of community" inside.

Hughes Group Architects

University of Virginia
Aquatic & Fitness Center
Charlottesville, Virginia

Thomas Jefferson's legendary Georgian-style Rotunda and "academic village" remain the proud heart of the University of Virginia, the institution he established at Charlottesville in 1819. Now, a new, award-winning facility is satisfying a critical function the nation's third president envisioned in 1785, saying, "Give about two hours everyday to exercise, for health must not be sacrificed to learning. A strong body makes the mind strong." The three-level, 150,000-square foot Aquatic & Fitness Center, designed by Hughes Group Architects, acts as the centerpiece of the University's distributed recreation program. Its Neoclassical brick-clad structure enhances its site through efficient planning, yet honors its campus by articulating major program components as individual forms. Thanks to a unique, two-story fitness spine that combines fitness activities and circulation with direct exposure to an adjacent plaza designed to host social events, the space is easily navigated by visitors heading for such activity areas as the aquatic zone, gymnasiums, fitness track, distributed locker rooms and cubicles, and administrative offices. Could Mr. Jefferson have foretold that the Center would become the most visited building on campus today?

Above: Exterior

Top left: Fitness spine.

Upper left: Gymnasium.

Lower left: Competition pool.

Photography: Dan Cunningham.

Hughes Group Architects

Trinity University
Center for Women and Girls in Sports
Washington, DC

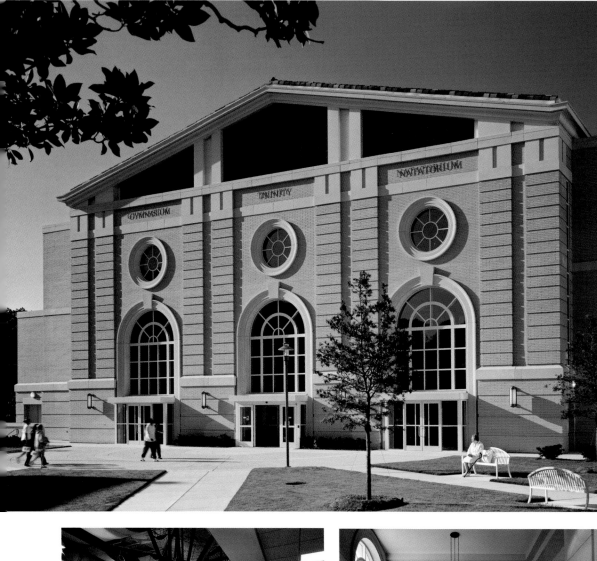

It is remarkable how a versatile new facility like the Center for Women and Girls in Sports at Trinity University, in Washington, DC can bring together an entire community Not only does the new four-level, 63,298-square foot space, designed by Hughes Group Architects, serve the nearly 2,000 students, the faculty and staff of the Catholic liberal arts college founded in 1897, it also welcomes thousands more in such community organizations as DC Scores, Girl Scout Council of the Nation's Capital, Washington Tennis and Education Foundation, and District of Columbia Public Schools. One key to its success is the integration of its architecture, a handsome, Neoclassical building featuring appropriate scale, rigorous proportions and fine detailing, with the existing campus fabric. In addition, the Center effectively houses such superb facilities as a 25-yard, six-lane swimming pool, fitness center, spa, dance/aerobics studio, indoor walking track and 1,600-seat main arena/basketball court, along with six outdoor tennis courts and an NCAA-competition field for soccer, field hockey and lacrosse. Trinity's pride is also the community's joy.

Top: Exterior.

Above left: Arena/basketball court.

Above right: Entrance lobby.

Photography: Dan Cunningham.

Jack L. Gordon Architects, PC AIA

345 Seventh Avenue
New York, NY 10001
212.279.0550
212.279.4015 (Fax)
www.jlgordon.com

Jack L. Gordon Architects, PC, AIA

KeySpan Park
Coney Island, Brooklyn, New York

Top: Playing field.

Above: Ticket windows and team store.

Left: Exterior on Surf Avenue.

Photography: Peter Paige, Cristo Holloway/Clockwork Apple Inc.

Forty-four years without baseball in Brooklyn, New York came to a triumphant end on June 25, 2001 when the Brooklyn Cyclones, a Triple A affiliate of the New York Mets, won their first home game in KeySpan Park, a new, 8,700-seat, 145,850-square foot base-ball stadium, designed by Jack L. Gordon Architects. Not only did the most popu-lous borough in New York City—home to 2.47 million residents (2000 Census)—have a winning team to replace the beloved Brooklyn Dodgers, who departed for Los Angeles in 1957. Coney Island, birthplace of America's earliest urban amusement parks, including

Steeplechase Park (1897), Luna Park (1903) and Dreamland Park (1904), could finally boast of a major attraction to revive its fabled entertainment district. This modern, sophisticated yet playful ballpark, located on Coney Island's legendary Boardwalk adjacent to the Atlantic Ocean and the land-mark Parachute Jump, suc-ceeds as a sports venue with attractive, functional and cost-effective facilities that please athletes, spectators and staff alike. Its features include general seating, pre-mium suites, party terrace and outfield bleachers that all enjoy excellent views of the playing field and beyond, a main concourse

Jack L. Gordon Architects, PC, AIA

Above: Main concourse.

Left: Outfield and Coney Island view.

Right: General seating and premium suites.

with concessions and other guest services that overlooks the field and keeps fans in sight of friends and families. Also included are up-to-date locker rooms, batting cages, press accommodations and other support spaces, and a team store, museum and retail spaces that draw both fans and residents. In addition, the stadium has won the affection of the community by acknowledging the historic nature of the site, including Coney Island's existing amusement park and other local businesses, with award-winning architecture that embodies the neighborhood's festive spirit. This is all capped by distinctive, neon-outlined event lights that are now regarded as hallmarks of the contemporary landscape, and continued access between Surf Avenue, the main thoroughfare, and the Boardwalk. When the Brooklyn Cyclones recently declared, "We are proud and grateful that KeySpan Park is considered one of the game's true jewels," they could have been speaking for Brooklyn as well.

To give students and alumni of the College of New Jersey a memorable gathering place to share experiences on its 289-acre, tree-lined campus in Ewing, Jack L. Gordon Architects was recently invited to expand and modernize its Brower Student Center, and to design a new, multi-purpose, 100,000-square foot Event Center to be attached to the existing structure. The College, founded in 1855 as the Garden State's first teacher training school, has evolved into a multi-purpose institution enrolling some 6,600 undergraduate and graduate students without having a signature building where students and alumni could assemble for sports, cultural and social events. The Event Center should enhance campus life the moment it opens. Resembling several facilities under one roof, the Collegiate Georgian-style building will host concerts, drama and more, along with Division III basketball and wrestling, in its fully-equipped arena, while supporting smaller-scale activities in its conference rooms, lounges and food service concession areas, aided by a newly improved kitchen and cafeteria in the adjoining space—a home away from home for past and present students.

Jack L. Gordon Architects, PC, AIA — Tradition Field
Port St. Lucie, Florida

While 20 years can make a profound difference for a baseball player, the consequences can be nearly as dramatic for a baseball stadium like Tradition Field, home of the New York Mets during spring training at Port St. Lucie, Florida. The 1980s structure had struggled with problems of capacity, amenities, appearance and back-of-house facilities. Now, with additional floor area and facilities wrapped around the existing structure in an innovative renovation by Jack L. Gordon Architects, the 7,000-seat, 124,816-square foot stadium offers fans and players a rewarding, new experience. Everything has fresh appeal, including general seating, premium suites, party and picnic terraces, concessions, berm area, team store, offices, lockers, toilets, aquatic training suite and elevators, installed for accessibility. Appreciating the difference, the New York Mets praise the design team for "its ability to listen carefully to our needs and to produce functional and creative solutions in our new and remodeled facilities."

Top: Entrance.
Above: Picnic terrace.
Left: Aquatic therapy pool.
Photography: Richard Mikeo.

Mojo • Stumer Architects

14 Plaza Road
Greenvale, NY 11548
516.625.3344
516.625.3418 (Fax)
www.mojostumer.com

Mojo • Stumer Architects

Equinox Scarsdale
Scarsdale, New York

Top: Exterior.
Left: Locker rooms.
Far left: Reception.
Opposite: Exercise room.
Photography: Phillip Ennis.

From one location to 30 plus, Equinox Fitness Clubs has grown vigorously, from a family business founded in 1991 to a chain in metropolitan New York, metropolitan Chicago, California and Florida. Its emphasis on comprehensive programs, attentive service and beautiful environments is popular wherever it goes, as shown by Equinox Scarsdale in suburban New York. Here, a two-level, 25,000-square foot facility, designed by Mojo Stumer Architects, offers members workout areas, exercise room, locker rooms, daycare facility and café, combining inexpensive, durable materials with sleek, cutting-edge design in a way few rivals could challenge.

A young, trendy and demanding population residing in Manhattan's Upper East Side keeps retail merchants, restaurateurs and consumer services wide-eyed, well equipped and accommodating to compete for customers. However, Equinox 54th Street is a five-level, 35,000-square foot fitness club, designed by Mojo-Stumer Architects, with a hidden handicap: three of its levels are underground. New Yorkers are not especially fond of shopping anywhere above or below street level, so the award-winning design tantalizes them by presenting an airy and open environment inside Equinox's conspicuous, two-story glass exterior wall on Second Avenue. Not only does the scheme turn the ground floor and mezzanine into a three-dimensional billboard sign for Equinox, it carefully follows through with bright, spacious and imaginatively lighted below-grade floors to draw members to such facilities as work out areas, exercise rooms, lap pool, spa, spinning room, lockers, and juice bar. Consequently, many area residents love what they see at Equinox 54th Street—and sign up.

Mojo • Stumer Architects

Boca Rio Golf Club
Boca Raton, Florida

If wine and cheese improve with age, consider what time has meant to Boca Raton's Boca Rio Golf Club. Having designed a challenging golf course for Boca Rio in 1967, master golf course architect Robert von Hagge proceeded to update it and raise the stakes for golfers in 1992, producing 195 magnificent acres of undulating greens, well-bunkered and tree-lined fairways, and a handful of formidable water hazards. Now, Boca Rio has a clubhouse designed by Mojo-Stumer Architects worthy of the exceptional quality of its course, thanks to an award-winning, 9,500-square foot renovation, of the existing, 18,000-square foot facility. The makeover, encompassing the reception area, main gallery, lounge, bar, dining room and card room, has made a time-worn setting into a more modern, sophisticated and friendly environment. Members catch a hint of this transformation on the exterior, where existing storefront-style windows with aluminum frames have been exchanged for new residential-style units framed in mahogany. Once they enter the clubhouse, they are surrounded by interiors that have been thoroughly studied and updated to provide a satisfying experience that meets contemporary

Above: Stairs from main gallery to locker rooms.

Right: Offices.

Opposite: Main gallery.

Photography: Brantley Photography.

Mojo • Stumer Architects   Boca Rio Golf Club
Boca Raton, Florida

Top: Lounge.
Above: Phone booth.
Left: Bar seating area.

standards. Of course, the colors, textures and furnishings now reflect today's preferences. Yet many changes have been subtler and possibly more significant. In one instance, the stair from the main gallery to the locker rooms below has been screened from immediate view by a ledge that serves as a backdrop for the central seating area. In the clubhouse as well as on the golf course, the little things can count as much as the big ones.

Rossetti

Two Towne Square
Suite 200
Southfield, MI 48076
248.262.8300
248.262.8360 (Fax)

www.rossetti.com

999 N. Sepulveda
Suite 100
El Segundo, California 90245
310.416.9660
310.416.9650 (Fax)

500 First Zhongshan Road So.
Suite 27C
Luwan District, Shanghai 200023
PR China
011.86.21.63037312.630.343.12
011.86.21.63037312.630.556.61 (Fax)

Rossetti

Old Dominion University
Ted Constant Convocation Center
Norfolk, Virginia

University Village, a 75-acre development highlighted by a sports/event venue, shopping center, restaurants, theaters, offices, research labs and residences, progressed from dream to reality at Old Dominion University, in Norfolk, Virginia, with the recent completion of the Ted Constant Convocation Center as the cornerstone. This 8,600-seat, 218,000-square foot arena, designed by Rossetti in association with Moseley Architects, has been developed to showcase such University events as convocations, Monarchs/Lady Monarchs basketball, concerts and family entertainment. Rossetti worked closely with the Athletic Department and various stakeholder groups during the planning and design process to ensure that the program and resulting design solution responded to each group's unique needs. A flexible facility that can be configured for a variety of uses through an innovative retractable seating system, the Center also includes a University Hall of Fame, 12 hospitality suites, President's Suite, conference facilities and retail space as well as locker rooms, strength/training rooms, team facilities and athletic offices. The "Ted", as it is known locally, is a major milestone in completing University Village, which has provided both the University and City of Norfolk with increased exposure and activity.

Above: Arena.

Left: Hall of Fame.

Lower left: Suite level at main entry.

Opposite: Main entrance.

Photography: Steve Maylone/Maylone Photography.

Rossetti

Home Depot National Training Center
at California State University
Dominguez Hills, California

Right: Athletes training center.
Below: Aerial view of stadium.
Lower left: Tennis stadium.
Lower right: Main entrance.
Opposite: Soccer stadium.
Photography: Benny Chan/Fotoworks, Tim Street-Porter.

At first glance, it is evident that Home Depot National Training Center at California State University, Dominguez Hills is a sports complex at harmony with its surroundings. Extensive landscaping leads patrons from parking to the entrance of the 27,000-seat soccer stadium, where their gaze is directed upward from the earth and masonry walls to the exposed steel structure supporting an elegant white, Teflon®-coated fiberglass canopy. The roof captures the stadium's vibrant atmosphere, amplifying the sound of the game without disturbing the neighborhood, while night lighting establishes a sophisticated mood for evening events. Rossetti's challenge was to transform 125 acres at CSUDH's Carson campus into the nation's most complete training facility for Olympic, amateur and professional athletes. The solution, which also includes a 13,000-seat tennis stadium, 20,000-seat track and field facility and accommodations for baseball, basketball, cycling, volleyball and other sports, creates a new archetype for sports.

Rossetti

Van Andel Arena
Grand Rapids, Michigan

Top left: Entrance lobby.

Above left: Arena.

Above right: Main Entrance.

Photography: Balthazar Korab/Korab Hedrich Blessing.

The spirit of over 200 enthusiastic private citizens in Grand Rapids, Michigan can be sensed at award-winning, 12,000-seat Van Andel Arena, designed by Rossetti. Determined to revitalize a depressed section of the business district while upgrading an adjacent historic district, they launched a grass-roots campaign to develop the facility. To build consensus, the Rossetti design team conducted public discussions and presentations with government officials, businesses, churches and other interested civic groups, meeting with community leaders to incorporate their experience and knowledge of the area's cultural heritage in their planning and design. Van Andel also represented state-of-the-art facilities, techniques and appointments. Its innovative structural system lowered the facility's profile to fit the scale and character of its neighborhood, yet left space for a dramatic, 60-foot high glass curtain wall, providing cityscape views from within and an active environment for traffic passing on game days, and plenty of room for basketball's CBA Hoops and hockey's IHL Griffins to call home. To accommodate future expansion, the back wall of the family deck was designed to be easily knocked out to permit an extension with extra seats. Van Andel's legacy lives on in the continued development that has resurrected downtown Grand Rapids.

Rossetti

Ford Field Stadium
Detroit, Michigan

The directive to Rossetti was straightforward yet demanding: Design Ford Field as a state-of-the-art, 65,000-seat venue for the NFL's Detroit Lions while integrating the structure into the urban fabric of downtown Detroit. The design team started by digging deep, setting the field 45 feet below grade to reduce the building's scale. Glass was used generously in all areas to provide daylight and outdoor views, highlighted by a giant, urban window at the southwest corner, 150 feet long and 90 feet high, to provide dramatic skyline views from the field and lower bowl seating, and views of the interior from the surrounding neighborhood. Ford Field also connects with its urban site by incorporating the adjacent, historic Hudson's Warehouse, creating space for the construction of over 500,000 square feet of street-level retail shopping, offices and entertainment facilities, and removing portions of the floors to create multi-story atriums that vertically divide the stadium functions from the office and retail spaces. This approach saved some $30 million over all-new construction and maintained the facades of the landmark warehouse, enabling Ford Field to function as a bridge between historic Detroit and contemporary Detroit.

Top left: Stadium Façade.

Top right: Adams St. food court .

Above: Atrium meets bowl.

Left: Interior Bowl.

Photography: Justin Maconochie.

119

Rossetti

USTA National Tennis Center
Flushing, New York

Right: Crowds on stairs.

Below: Aerial view of site.

Bottom right: Seating bowl in Arthur Ashe Stadium.

Photography: Justin Maconochie.

The World's Fairs of 1940 are gone, but New York City's Flushing Meadows-Corona Park thrives with the Unisphere and such lively tenants as the 46-acre USTA National Tennis Center. The Center was designed by Rossetti to comprise a new 22,000-seat tennis Stadium Arthur Ashe stadium and, a remodeled 10,000-seat Stadium, and such new features as 36 outdoor tennis courts, a 1,500-seat food court, and a nine-court indoor tennis facility. To complement the natural setting with "tennis in the park," the Rossetti design team created a fully landscaped environment where Arthur Ashe Stadium arose on a red brick base with a pattern of regular, square-punched windows, enclosing such spaces as players' lounges, offices, restaurants and press facilities while reflecting the urban setting of the Queens neighborhood. In turn, the branch-like tubular structure supporting the upper seating bowl echoed the tree-lined avenues of the park ringing the site, and the open concourse encompassing the seating bowl afforded sweeping vistas of the field courts, the park and New York City. For all its links to the outside world, the Center projected a powerful identity of its own from the start, based on a landscape of lush planting beds, hedgerows and trees, a formal geometry that reflected the park's Beaux Arts layout, and unique massing and materials that are instantly recognizable to on-site patrons and an international population of telecast viewers.

Sasaki Associates, Inc.

54 Pleasant Street
Watertown, MA 02472
617.926.3300
617.924.2748 (Fax)
www.sasaki.com

Sasaki Associates, Inc.

Sasaki Associates, Inc.

Johns Hopkins University
Ralph S. O'Connor Recreation Center
Baltimore, Maryland

Even non-athletes like to work out, a frequently overlooked need that inspired Baltimore's Johns Hopkins University, founded in 1876 as one of the Western Hemisphere's first research institutions, to develop the new, three-level, 65,000-square foot Ralph S. O'Connor Recreation Center. Clad in brick, limestone and glass, the award-winning structure, designed by Sasaki Associates, serves as an addition to the existing main athletic facility and provides a foundation for the University's recreational athletics program serving 4,000 students at the Homewood campus. Non-athletes can gather here to enjoy such facilities as the multi-use gymnasium for basketball, volleyball and badminton, 165-meter, four-lane jogging track, 30-foot climbing wall and four racquetball courts (two convertible to squash courts), as well as the weight room, fitness center and three multi-purpoose rooms, which are contained inside the glass and brick-enclosed pavilion at the entrance. Anyone with a fear of heights can still enjoy watching classmates scale the Center's climbing wall—from the comfort of an upper level balcony, anyway.

Top: Main staircase.

Above: Multi-purpose gymnasium.

Right: Climbing wall.

Opposite: Exterior.

Sasaki Associates, Inc.

Loyola College
Fitness and Aquatic Center
Baltimore, Maryland

When Loyola College in Maryland, a Jesuit Catholic university founded in 1852, recently completed a new, two-story, 115,000-square foot Fitness and Aquatic Center for its 6,156 undergraduate and graduate students, it envisioned a facility whose goals looked simultaneously forward and backward. To design a high quality building that would endure for years, Sasaki Associates emphasized aesthetics, durability and ease of maintenance. On the other hand, to maintain the unique character of the campus, which was originally an estate, the architect located the Center on the site of a previous structure. Now that the Center is open, students are finding much to like inside, including a 25-yard, eight-lane pool, three-court gymnasium, multi-purpose activity court, elevated jogging track, racquet and squash courts, 6,000-square foot fitness center, group exercise rooms, 30-foot climbing wall and administrative offices. Rick Satterlee, vice president for student development at Loyola, reports, "Over 90 percent of our undergraduates use the facility on a regular basis."

Top: 25-yard pool.

Above: Exterior.

Left: Cafe.

Opposite: Entrance lobby.

Photography: Maxwell Mackenzie (top, opposite) Greg Hursley (left, above).

Sasaki Associates, Inc.

University of California Santa Barbara Recreation Center and Aquatic Complex
Santa Barbara, California

Above: Entrances to various activity areas.

Right: 25-yard pool.

Below: Phase II expansion.

Opposite: Exterior of main gymnasium.

Once a small, independent teachers' college, University of California, Santa Barbara has grown vigorously since 1944 as part of the UC system, currently serving 19,799 students on a 989-acre campus. UCSB's award-winning, 120,000-square foot Recreation Center and Aquatics Complex, designed by Sasaki Associates and constructed in Phases I and II, is an ambitious response to students' diverse interests. The village-like cluster of facilities, connected through interior or protected exterior circulation, includes a 24,000-square foot multi-court gymnasium, six racquetball courts, two squash courts, weight room, locker rooms, offices and support spaces, along with such aquatic facilities as a 50 meter x 25 yard x 30 meter L-shaped pool with diving well and diving boards, and a 25-yard pool with attached 0- to 3-foot depth teaching area and handicap access ramp. The recent Phase II expansion adds a

Sasaki Associates, Inc.

multi-activities court, cardio/weight room, climbing wall, multi-purpose rooms, locker rooms, offices and classroom. Confirming the UCSB Student Handbook's claim that "Physical activity can help relieve stress and loosen up those tense muscles, clear the brain-fog caused by too much studying, and offer great opportunities for meeting people and making friends," students keep the "Rec-Cen" active at all hours.

Top: Racquetball and squash courts area.

Above: Locker rooms.

Left: Multi-court gymnasium.

Souto Moura Arquitectos, Lda

Rua da Alegria
Parque Habitacional do Lima
Ent. 29 - Hab. 1C
4200-024 Porto
Portugal
351.22.5505153 (Tel/Fax)

Souto Moura Arquitectos, Lda

Braga Stadium
Braga, Portugal

B2

Rising like a force of nature from Monte Castro in the Portuguese city of Braga's Dume Sports Park, the new, 30,000-seat Braga Municipal Stadium, designed by Eduardo Souto de Moura of Souto Moura Arquitectos, is an astonishing consequence of Portugal's campaign to build or renovate 10 soccer stadiums for the 2004 UEFA European soccer championship games. The Stadium's two steeply raked tiers of seating overlook the playing field at the site of a former granite quarry. The southwest stand, being carved out of the hillside, erects its reinforced concrete structure on a foundation of bedrock, stairs, elevators, concourses and light shafts, while the northeast stand rests on sharply cantilevered reinforced concrete piers that collectively resemble a ship's hull. Of course, the space between the stands easily generates a drama of its own. At ground level, soccer is played on a field covering multiple layers of underground parking and players' facilities, remaining free of seating at the end zones—a towering wall of granite faces one end and a landscaped hillside the other—unlike traditional stadiums. Above the stands, a lightweight roof of ribbed metal panels suspended on

Above: Concourse.

Opposite: Southwest stand and granite hillside.

First overleaf: Playing field facing northeast stand.

Second overleaf: Stadium in profile.

Photography: Paul Raftery/ VIEW, Christian Richters.

Souto Moura Arquitectos, Lda　Braga Stadium
Braga, Portugal

Souto Moura Arquitectos, Lda   Braga Stadium
Braga, Portugal

a network of steel tensile cables, inspired by Inca rope bridges Souto de Moura observed during a trip to Peru, protects the spectators and gains lateral stability from V-section trusses that support stadium lighting and channel rainwater to cantilevered water troughs. Tourists to Braga, an historic city founded in 300 B.C. by the Celts and famed for the splendid churches that mark its long-standing role as Portugal's religious center, have wasted no time adding the Stadium to their itineraries.

Above: Suspended roof.

Left: Beneath the southwest stand.

136

The Day When Everybody Wins

By Roger Yee

Creating great experiences for everyone—athletes, non-athletes, spectators and staff—is emerging as a winning strategy for designing today's best sports and recreational facilities.

"Winning isn't everything; it's the only thing."

You don't have to be Tiger Woods, Lance Armstrong or Michelle Kwan to know what legendary Green Bay Packers coach Vince Lombardi meant when he quoted (and thus immortalized) Vanderbilt and UCLA football coach Henry "Red" Sanders. Of course, keeping score is more complicated in the game of life. Not only is there more than one way to win, there is more to life than winning—a point Lombardi himself emphasized—and even non-athletes can enjoy sports and recreation. To make athletic activity more widely available, the United States has been engaged in a building boom that began unofficially on April 6, 1992, the opening day of Baltimore's Oriole Park at Camden Yards.

Go to a ballgame and promote economic growth and community development too? It's possible at Dr. Pepper/7-Up Ballpark, Frisco, TX, designed by David M. Schwarz/Architectural Services.

significant revenues, which the U.S. Census Bureau has estimated as $20.22 billion for spectator sports and $45.82 billion for recreational industries. The impact of the new, user-friendly and hospitality-oriented approach to the design of sports and recreational facilities is not hard to spot, starting with the many Major League Baseball stadiums that have been built or heavily remodeled since 1992.

Of course, Camden Yards is not the only inspiration for America's new sports and recreational facilities. While some design trends reflect changes within the national and international sports organizations that set standards for their games, others express society's evolving attitudes about sports. Consider the following cultural phenomena and their impact.

A state-of-the-art stadium designed by HOK in the image of such revered early 20th century predecessors as Boston's Fenway Park, Chicago's Wrigley Field and New York's Polo Grounds, Camden Yards demonstrated that a modern sports venue could do considerably more than provide a good playing field and seating bowl. It revitalized downtown Baltimore and sent a powerful message to businesses and municipalities across the nation: Sports and architecture could jointly promote economic growth and community development. By creating a ballpark that regarded basic, functional spaces, minimal creature comforts and activities focused solely on the game merely as a starting point, the Orioles improved the performance, safety and morale of athletes, and enhanced the convenience, comfort and entertainment of spectators.

Any major change in the character of America's sports and recreation can have considerable impact on our society. After all, there are 30 million amateur athletes playing sports, 55 million fitness enthusiasts following exercise programs, 38 million spectators attending sports events, and millions of fans following the action by television and radio. Their enthusiasm generates

Everyone in the pool: How the demographics of sports are expanding

"Our society now believes athletic activity should be part of your entire life," says Don Dissinger, AIA, senior vice president of EwingCole, an architecture firm based in Philadelphia that counts many sports and recreational projects in its various portfolios. "You start working out as a child, maybe traveling with your soccer team as early as age seven, and stay active in high school, college and work, right up through retirement and continuing care." Consequently, new facilities are being designed to open space, staff and equipment to girls and women, amateur athletes and non-athletes, and toddlers and seniors, as well as boys and male athletes.

The enactment of Title IX in 1971, requiring schools to give girls and women access to sports and sports facilities traditionally focused on boys and men, has produced highly visible results over time. For example, California's Fresno State University spent over $15 million on state-of-the-art athletic facilities for men and some $300,000 on athletic facilities for women prior to Title IX. It subsequently devoted more than $8 million in construction to establish equity for women, including a new, 2,500-seat stadium for its champion women's Bulldog Softball team.

Tomorrow's "active seniors," 64 million Baby Boomers who start turning 60 in 2006, also expect sports and recreation to help rewrite the conventional script for retirement. "Boomers are changing expectations about what 65-year-olds should be doing," observes Craig Bouck, a principal of Barker Rinker Seacat, a Denver architecture firm helping many communities develop recreational facilities. "Their parents like things old fashioned. But Boomers will soon have leisure time on their hands, and don't want to spend it passively in places like today's senior centers." Bouck anticipates that most senior centers will be converted to recreational centers, financed and equipped for health and wellness through Boomers' overwhelming political and economic clout.

Natatoriums for all, from toddlers to seniors, are typical of new municipal facilities like the Paul Derda Recreational Center, Broomfield, CO, designed by Barker Rinker Seacat Architecture.

Corporate relocation consultants say young families with children are drawn to cities and towns with amenities such as the Paul Derda Recreational Center, which is considered a hallmark of quality.

Chasing the action before and after the game: Where hospitality is reshaping sports venues

With the hospitality and entertainment industries raising the standards of comfort, safety, technology and aesthetics for customers across the world, it's not surprising that other leisure-oriented businesses are following suit. In fact, the sports world has probably learned as much from Walt Disney as it has from the Baltimore Orioles about improving the customer experience through graduated price points for seating, quality food services, retail shops and other concessions, multi-media programming, ample toilets with changing tables, secure zones for shared facilities, sports museums and halls of fame, and shiny façades designed by star architects. Today's sports and recreational facilities promote an ever-expanding menu of amenities and activities.

"The new stadiums are better loved than those of the 1960s and 1970s," declares Tom Greene, a principal of David M. Schwarz/Architectural Services, an architecture firm in Washington, D.C. with considerable experience in professional sports facilities. "Everyone loves the oldest stadiums, such as Wrigley and Fenway, but most of those from the 1960s and 1970s were cheaply done and showed it. Today's facilities are for the fans, and they're more complex, offering more ways to spend money and have a good time."

Obviously, it takes money to brighten a day at the stadium or recreational center, which leads private and public developers to seek fresh sources of financing and fees that ultimately affect their design. Corporate sponsorship of professional sports venues is nothing new, even though the current passion for naming rights—producing such unfamiliar-sounding places as Citizens

Bank Park (Philadelphia Phillies), U.S. Cellular Field (Chicago White Sox), and Petco Park (San Diego Padres)—is only one of many means for team owners to upgrade facilities and pay star athletes. For better or worse, big business is likely to embrace additional opportunities to "brand" the fan experience as they arise.

On the other hand, creative new alliances are underwriting many non-profit sports and recreational facilities. "Partnerships between communities and hospitals work by letting hospitals offer such services as cardiac rehabilitation in community recreational centers they

Unlike the big pro sports venues of the 1960s and 1970s, modern examples like the Philadelphia Phillies' Citizens Bank Park, designed by EwingCole, strive for a satisfying spectator experience.

don't have to build themselves," states Chris Chivetta, principal-in-charge of Philadelphia-based Hastings & Chivetta Architects, which designs sports facilities for communities, colleges and universities. When schools and communities share facilities, he adds, joint occupancy can succeed when such issues as scheduling and security are carefully addressed.

Couch potatoes, throw off your cushions: Why schools and communities are focusing on sports for quality of life

Quality of life may not be the primary concern of a prospective college student, or the main reason why a home buyer moves into town. However, schools and communities have gotten the message: Quality of life is critical to success. Having observed how exercise, conditioning and sports appear to play major physical and emotional roles in maintaining a high quality of life, schools are developing appropriate facilities to appeal to non-athletes as well as athletes, just as cities and towns are building one-stop recreational centers for every citizen regardless of age or sex.

What activities keep a recreational facility busy day and night? According to Chivetta, staying in touch with constituents provides the best answers. "In planning a recreational center, you survey a cross section of the population—the sports staff, sports clubs, Greeks, student government, community groups and elected officials—to identify what people want," he reports. "Flexibility and versatility are critical over the long term.

Giving fans attractive reasons to have a good time before, during and even after the game, as shown in Citizens Bank Park, strengthens the appeal of sports to families and businesses.

Students don't visit Georgia Tech's Campus Recreation Center just to work out, and features such as this inviting café turn the building into a campus social center where everyone likes to gather.

Sports go in and out of favor. Right now, racquet ball courts are being converted for wally ball, spinning and other uses."

No matter what they elect to do, athletes and non-athletes increasingly want pleasing physical environments around them. Their faith in good design is measurable. While college recruiters credit exceptional sports and recreational facilities for student enrollment and alumni generosity, corporate relocation consultants value them as hallmarks of desirable communities.

Outstanding athletic facilities command attention even outside the Big Ten campuses, which historically field many of America's finest collegiate football and basketball teams. Georgia Institute of Technology ends campus tours at the new Campus Recreation Center to exploit its dynamic image. No less an elite institution than Stanford University has proudly won the coveted Sears Directors' Cup for the nation's best overall NCAA Division I collegiate athletic program ten years in a row—and operates impressive sports facilities to keep coaches and athletes solidly in the win column.

Wait 'til next year

Much of the improvement in sports and recreational facility design is evolutionary, as building products manufacturers indicate. "Locker rooms are getting more color, better finishes and new flexibility to handle diverse populations," reports Jim Dougherty, vice president, sales for Crossville Ceramics, a major ceramic tile maker. Dusty trophy cases are yielding to new, multi-media and interactive sports museums and halls of fame in both professional and collegiate sports venues. "Preserving sports history enriches the experience for alumni and other fans, recruits athletes and prevents young people from losing their heritage," notes Jerry Murphy, president of Murphy & Orr Exhibits, which works with commercial and academic sports clients.

Yet there's always room for new ideas. The development of reliable, low-cost LED technology, for example, is ushering in

Since exercise and sports improve life for everyone on campus, Georgia Institute of Technology, Atlanta, GA, developed this Campus Recreation Center, designed by Hastings & Chivetta Architects.

Professional sports teams can thrive in communities without having to be major league franchises, as demonstrated by KeySpan Park, Brooklyn, NY, designed by Jack L. Gordon Architects.

a new generation of scoreboards and display screens at sports venues that supply great images and plenty of data to spectators wherever they are. "Fans like them because they're not static," points out Mark Steinkamp, spokesman for Daktronics, a major producer of LED-based signage. "Advertisers like them since they allow messages to be crafted for specific times and places." And sports flooring can now be specified that conforms to sustainable design principles of the Green Building Council. According to Jon Isaacs, vice president, sales for Connor Sports Flooring, "Our SmartWood program uses maple from managed forests, and we've formed a strategic alliance with Nike to recycle its rubber for the pads we place under our synthetic floors."

Many questions inevitably arise about the future of sports and recreational facilities. Will the public demand and get better pre- and post-season use of lavish professional sports palaces financed by taxes and bonds? Will stratification of ticket prices and spectator accommodations lead to social discord? Will academic sports facilities emulate their professional counterparts in complexity and cost? The answers to these and other uncertainties will play out over time.

Still, there are few events as exciting in modern life as those we witness at sports and recreational venues. They may be momentary interruptions of a 9-to-5 existence that we cannot—and probably do not—want to escape. Nevertheless, who would have predicted that a Hawaiian teenage golf phenomenon like Michelle Wie would turn pro on her 16th birthday, shortly after defeating numerous experienced, grown male players at the quarterfinals of the U.S. Amateur Public Links Championship in July 2005?

See you at the game!

As collegians increasingly balance scholarship with athletic activity, facilities like George Mason University's Aquatic and Fitness Center, Fairfax, VA, designed by Hughes Group Architects, could proliferate.

National Intramural-Recreational Sports Association

Outstanding Sports Facilities Award Winners for 2002, 2004 and 2005

Introduction

Sports, fitness and wellness programs have become a way of life for millions of Americans because of the known health benefits. College and university campuses all over the country encourage this trend by building new, dynamic recreational sports facilities, or renovating old facilities, and providing programs for students, faculty and the surrounding community.

A 2004 survey by the National Intramural-Recreational Sports Association (NIRSA) reveals that from 2004 to 2010, 333 U.S. campuses plan to collectively spend approximately $3.17 billion on new construction or renovation, at an average building cost of $14.2 million. This growth will provide an additional 2.15 million college students with facilities where they can exercise and participate in campus recreational sports and programs. University regents and chancellors encourage this construction—whether paid for with student's fees, legislated state monies, bonds, or through private funding—because they recognize the value to students' overall wellbeing and satisfaction. The pecuniary bottom line is that state-of-the-art recreational sports facilities, with their sports, fitness and wellness programs, attract and retain students and faculty in the highly competitive arena of higher education recruitment.

Since 1988, when NIRSA began presenting annual Outstanding Sports Facilities Awards for creative, innovative designs of new or expanded facilities, 92 winners have been chosen and published as a resource for campus master planners, recreational sports directors, designers, architects, contractors, and recreational sports students.

The awards selection is time consuming, the eligibility requirements are stringent, and the competition is keen. On average, 20 facilities compete each year for this award, with 7-10 selected as winners. To be eligible, the facility must be a NIRSA Institutional Member, total construction costs (excluding design and land fees) must be a minimum of $2 million, and the facility must be more than 20,000 square feet.

The judges are recreational sports directors from Member Institutions, and Associate Members who are designers/architects. They consider the applicants architectural design and aesthetics—a demonstrated sense of beauty or good taste—both inside and outside of the building, as well as the site itself. Applicants must describe to the judges how the facility achieves its planned usage, how it accommodates the volume of anticipated participation, and how they allocated resources to the usable spaces.

The judges also evaluate the facility's functionality in terms of operations and the delivery of programs, events, services, and other uses. Applicants must describe how the facility achieves the efficient use of space and how spatial adjacencies contribute to the overall day-to-day operation of the facility. They describe how the ancillary/support areas contribute to functional efficiency, and how the materials/finishes demonstrate consistencies within the scope of the project. They explain specifics such as the location of control points, if the facility is user-friendly, if any incorporated energy conservation is measured, how the necessary security, life safety, and ADA-related code requirements were included, and how they incorporated the maintenance and operation expenses into the design.

The architectural design—the overall aesthetics—is a crucial part of the competition. Competitors might describe how the exterior design of the facility complements and incorporates the campus' master plan. Designers might detail how the facility achieves sensitivity and compliance for environmental issues, what innovative use of construction techniques, color schemes, textures, plants, finishes, and lighting

By doubling its size and enlivening its design, the newly expanded Student Recreation Center at the University of Alabama (Tuscaloosa) is drawing 3,000 students each day. Photography, Curtis Photographers.

(natural and artificial) contribute to the interior and exterior beauty of the facility, and if the quality of the building materials contribute to the aesthetics of the facility. Any unique features and noteworthy characteristics in function and design, unusual architectural features, the latest high-tech mechanical/electrical features, security systems, and energy management systems might also be pointed out.

NIRSA is proud to showcase the following 23 college and university campuses that won Outstanding Sports Facilities Awards during 2002, 2004 and 2005.

2005 Winners

- Student Recreation Center - University of Alabama (Tuscaloosa)
- Student Recreation Center - Boise State University
- Campus Recreation Center - Georgia Institute of Technology
- Colvin Recreation Center - Oklahoma State University (Stillwater)
- Dixon Recreation Center - Oregon State University
- Student Recreation Center - Sonoma State University
- Aquatic & Fitness Center - University of Virginia (Charlottesville)

2004 Winners

- University Recreation Center - Texas Christian University
- Recreation and Wellness Center - University of Central Florida
- Campus Recreation & Wellness Center - University of Houston
- Student Recreation Center - University of North Texas
- Strom Thurmond Wellness & Fitness Center - University of South Carolina
- Bryan Williams, M.D. Student Center - University of Texas Southwestern Medical Center at Dallas
- Wade King Student Recreation Center - Western Washington University

2002 Winners

- The Freeman Center - Christopher Newport University
- Student Recreation Center - Georgia State University
- Student Life Center - Fort Lewis College
- Fritz B. Burns Recreation Center - Loyola Marymount University (Los Angeles)
- Fitness and Aquatic Center - Loyola College in Maryland
- Student Recreation and Wellness Center - Kent State University
- St. Paul Gymnasium Renovation - University of Minnesota (Twin Cities)
- Student Recreation Center - Washington State University
- Student Recreation Center - West Virginia University

About NIRSA

NIRSA is the leading resource for professional and student development, education, and research in collegiate recreational sports. A non-profit membership organization, NIRSA directly impacts millions of people in higher education and accesses an international network of more than 4,000 highly trained Professional, Individual, and Institutional Members on over 650 campuses. Our Members manage the multimillion-dollar facilities you see here, as well as many others, with their large annual operating budgets and highly dedicated professional staffs.

The Association began in 1950 as the National Intramural Association (NIA) and was founded by Dr. William Wasson, a professor at Dillard University in New Orleans, who organized a meeting of 22 African-American men and women intramural directors from 11 Historically Black Colleges (HBCU's). The mission was to improve the quality of life of individuals and communities through the education and training of professionals in recreational sports, fitness, and wellness. The Association's name changed to the National Intramural-Recreational Sports Association in 1975.

If you would like to learn more about NIRSA, the work of the Association and our dedicated professionals, or membership, please visit our web site at www.nirsa.org.

Not only is the new Student Recreation Center for Georgia State University unlike any other building on the school's downtown Atlanta campus, it is also sleek, dynamic and clearly "fun" to use. Photography, Sam Fentress.

✴**NIRSA** Outstanding Sports Facilities Awards 2005

University of Alabama
Student Recreation Center
Tuscaloosa, Alabama

"Wow" is a common reaction when students enter the new 195,000-square foot Student Recreation Center at the University of Alabama (Tuscaloosa). The translucent skylight bathes the complex with a soft natural light, creating a welcoming atmosphere and visually unifying the entire interior. The $18.7-million new facility, nearly double its original size, offers 3,000 students a day the use of the group fitness rooms, weight/fitness areas, wellness and therapy suites, a family changing area, an outdoor leisure aquatics area, and a tennis complex. Architectural firms TMP Architects, Inc., and Sherlock, Smith and Adams with consultants Brailsford & Dunlavey, Counsilman Hunsaker, and Canning-Gonsoulin designed the facility with environmental sustainability in mind. Throughout, low-maintenance materials with low VOC content or recycled materials were used, as well as porcelain floor tile, durable wall coatings, and hand-made tiles that require no chemicals, adhesives or paints. "We are proud that the Student Recreation Center Complex is extremely inviting but it isn't just pretty," says George M. Brown, CRSS, Director of University Recreation. "It is a comprehensive, fun, functional, and user-friendly facility."

Top: Exterior.

Upper right: Pool.

Upper left: Gym with stairs.

Left: Lobby with the Cafe.

Opposite: Lobby.

Photography: Curtis Photographers.

Boise State University
Student Recreation Center
Boise, Idaho

Energy conservation was a key factor in the design by Yost Grube Hall Architecture and Design West Architects. The building's orientation—with solid walls to block the summer sun, shaded east windows, trees on the west side, high translucent glazing to reduce glare—all reduce high energy demands for air-conditioning. The transparency of the $12.5 million building, due to its openness and generous glass walls, floods the facility with daylight and invites the campus community inside at night. The program components contained in the 90,000-square foot building include: a 3-court gymnasium, outdoor rental center, wellness center, aerobics/dance studios, Wallyball, volleyball, badminton, racquetball and squash courts, kickboxing classes, lounge, 3,000-square foot exercise studio, two 1,500-square foot multipurpose rooms, elevated running track, nutritional counseling, personal training and massage. "The construction of this state-of-the-art fitness and recreation facility has literally changed the fabric of the campus…not simply replaced an older building," says Joyce A. Grimes, Executive Director, Campus Recreation.

Above: Illuminated exterior invites patrons inside.

Top right: A 1/11-mile jogging track.

Upper right: Entry plaza—a signature gateway.

Lower right: Cycling is popular.

Bottom right: Fitness and strength training area.

Opposite: Climbing wall provides challenges.

Photography: David Hursley.

✓NIRSA Outstanding Sports Facilities Awards 2005

Georgia Institute of Technology
Campus Recreation Center
Atlanta, Georgia

When Hastings & Chivetta Architects, Inc. designed the 300,000-square foot Campus Recreation Center at Georgia Institute of Technology, the challenge was to enclose the world-class outdoor pool built for the 1996 Summer Olympics, yet retain its original roof. Solution? Build ten 58-foot-tall "bridge" arches of post-tension concrete to span 175 feet over the old pool, creating the largest "column-less" indoor span in the country. This new top floor accommodates a 60,000-square foot gymnasium and numerous multi-purpose activities. As part of a long-term joint research project between Georgia Tech, Georgia Power, and the U.S. Department of Energy, the roof of the natatorium contains solar panels that provide 30 percent of the building's power. The new $43-million, energy-efficient fitness center houses racquetball courts, climbing wall, leisure pool and a 500-car three-level parking deck. "The Campus Recreation Center is the balance between usable space and the aesthetic element; it is functional, yet visually stimulating without extravagance," says Michael W. Edwards, Director of Campus Recreation.

Upper right: The Olympic pool is now inside.

Right: Top floor jogging track.

Below: Timeless colors used throughout.

Opposite: Clear glass captures indirect light.

Photography: Sam Fentress.

Oklahoma State University
Colvin Recreation Center
Stillwater, Oklahoma

"Turning the box inside-out" was the solution to the multitude of challenges faced by Allen Brown Architects and Moody-Nolan, Inc., consultants in the $20.7-million renovation of the Colvin Recreation Center at Oklahoma State University. The dynamic results improved the building's function and feel, and nearly doubled the recreational space for programs. "They turned a large, windowless 1960s brick box into a large open, vibrant activity center that is the pride of the entire campus," says Kent E. Bunker, CRSS, Director of Campus Recreation. The 210,750-square foot expansion adds more sport courts, jogging track, "virtual" golf, and three levels of fitness equipment rooms that overlook a

new outdoor courtyard with a year-round leisure pool. The new, renovated interior with its dynamic flow of space and visuals of all activities is appealing. A central staircase creates a natural circulation path from the lower main entry up through the top atrium.

Top: The new building as seen from the southeast.

Above: Gymnasium.

Right: The Aquatic Park remains open year-round.

Opposite: The main stairs provide activity views.

Photography: Joseph Mills.

NIRSA **Outstanding Sports Facilities Awards 2005**

Oregon State University
Dixon Recreation Center
Corvallis, Oregon

Above right: The entry is the Center's heart.

Above left: The main entry on South Campus.

Left: Spinning rooms have mountain views.

Far left: Running track is suspended over gym.

Opposite lower right: The climbing wall is very popular.

Photography: Pete Eckert.

"It just keeps getting better and better" could be a slogan for the Dixon Recreation Center at Oregon State University. Built in 1976, several renovations have expanded the facility that accommodates more than 3,000 students daily. The latest, a $20-million, 150,000-square foot addition/renovation, adds a three-court gymnasium, an 11-lap-per-mile running track, large multipurpose rooms, large weight room, wellness suite, and new outdoor recreation center.

Sustainability was a project focus for the facility. Designed by Yost Grube Hall Architecture, it is organized around a two-level, day-light-filled "circulation hall" that spans the existing buildings and provides natural lighting that reduces the need for electric lighting. OSU's first holistically designed and sustainable building employs natural ventilation to minimize mechanical cooling, durable exterior materials to reduce long-term maintenance, and native plants to reduce

water and harmful garden chemicals usage. "In 2005, the addition unified the multi-phased building into a single facility in terms of exterior architecture, interior circulation and finish quality," reports Thomas G. Kirch, Director of University Recreation.

NIRSA Outstanding Sports Facilities Awards 2005

Sonoma State University
Student Recreation Center
Rohnert Park, California

When Sonoma State University "re-imaged" its 1960s campus using sustainable materials, the $10.9-million renovated state-of-the-art Student Recreation Center was the first building completed. Built with environmentally friendly materials, the Center is an efficient, attractive facility that demonstrates a minimal impact on the environment, saves operational costs, and conveys a social statement. Using a mountain view as a dramatic natural backdrop, LPA Architects (an early member of the U.S. Green Building Council), Ellerbe Becket, and consultant Bill Manning designed the 59,538-square foot building to house new gymnasiums, elevated running track, multipurpose studios, fitness rooms, and more. "The use of sunlight and natural materials creates a warm, welcoming space for students," says Pamela M. Su, CRSS, Director of Campus Recreation. Throughout the facility, LPA chose eco-friendly products such as Alaskan yellow cedar, floor tiles made of recycled glass, metal roof, natural slate floor, certified cedar wood, recycled content carpeting, linoleum from linseed oil, and furniture made of recycled plastic, paper, glass and sunflower seeds.

Above: Facade at dusk.

Right: Second floor lookout.

Opposite left: Gymnasium.

Opposite upper right: Jogging track.

Opposite lower right: Weight room.

Photography: Cristian D. Costea Photography.

NIRSA Outstanding Sports Facilities Awards 2005

University of Virginia
Aquatic & Fitness Center
Charlottesville, Virginia

Keeping a look that reflects the historic fabric of the University of Virginia was a primary concern for Hughes Group Architects when it designed the new 150,000-square foot Aquatic & Fitness Center. The $26.5-million red brick and white "Jeffersonian" exterior, complete with columns, blends with other campus buildings in terms of scale and tight site constraints. The stately white columns are repeated within the interior in a space made even grander by the brilliant glow of natural light from a skylight that runs through the main lobby. Students and faculty use the 50-meter Olympic pool, three-court gymnasium, indoor walking/running track, multipurpose rooms, free weight space, cardio-vascular exercise and cycling classes and the family changing room. "More than five million people have used the AFC since it opened, upholding the Jeffersonian belief that 'a strong body makes the mind strong,'" says Mark E. Fletcher, CRSS, Director of Intramural Recreational Sports and Associate Athletic Director. "It has become the most visited building at the University."

Above: Interior lobby is a focal point.

Left: Gym.

Far left: Lobby.

Opposite upper left: Tree lights illuminate the south terrace.

Photography: Dan Cunningham.

Texas Christian University
University Recreation Center
Fort Worth, Texas

When architects Cannon Design and Hahnfeld, Hoffer and Standford designed the 232,500-square foot addition/renovation of the outdated 1970s Recreational Center at Texas Christian University, they transformed it and doubled its size. The $25.6-million addition includes an atrium lobby, three-court gymnasium, weight and fitness center, climbing wall, racquetball and squash courts, multipurpose rooms, and mezzanine-level running track, while the renovations include a remodeled gymnasium and refurbished natatorium. While aesthetics were important, funding was focused on function. Insulated glass reduces the need for excessive daytime lighting, and terrazzo, syn-thetic and tile floors reduce maintenance costs. The exterior design fits well with the conservative nature of the campus while including landmark qualities. The curved copper roof, the large glass expanse, colors and sport graphics are repeated throughout the facility, including the design of the outdoor leisure pool. "At TCU, we don't believe that one university can change the world," says Steve Kintigh, CRSS, Director of Campus Recreation, "but we do believe that healthy active students can. The URC is evidence of TCU's extraordinary commitment to this philosophy."

Above: Exterior blends with campus buildings.

Right: Spinning room seen from track.

Opposite upper right: Gym.

Opposite upper left: Lobby.

Opposite lower right: Climbing wall.

Opposite lower left: Pool.

Photography: Jon Miller, copyright Hedrich Blessing.

University of Central Florida
Recreation and Wellness Center
Orlando, Florida

The most distinguishing feature of the 84,000-square foot Recreation and Wellness Center at the University of Central Florida is its unique horizontal and vertical shape. Architects FBBA/RDG Group and consultant Walter Moore designed a cantilevering roof over the 100-foot x 400-foot trapezoidal. An angled column carries soffits off the roof, while aluminum panels match the tower's crown that encases a 41-foot climbing wall. All of the elements create a sense of drama for this campus landmark. The two-story weight room has a serpentine glass curtain wall that undulates in and out of brick piers. The two-story, $11.7-million Center features basketball, volleyball and badminton courts, weight/cardio training areas, six-lane outdoor pool, sandy beach bottom lagoon swimming pool, and nearby 18-hole disc golf course, and softball/baseball fields. "The Recreation and Wellness Center has exceeded everyone's expectation in its mission to enhance student's quality of life," says James Wilkening, CRSS, Associate Director of Recreational Sports and Programs. "It provides a valuable recruiting tool for the university."

Above: Wide horizontal brick accents exterior.

Right: Fitness room.

Far right: Gym viewed from jogging track.

Opposite upper left: Corridor.

Photography: RDG Planning & Design, copyright Assassi Productions.

NIRSA Outstanding Sports Facilities Awards 2004

University of Houston
Campus Recreation & Wellness Center
Houston, Texas

In Texas, "It's not braggin' if'en it's true." The gigantic Campus Recreation & Wellness Center at the University of Houston boasts the largest collegiate pool, one of the highest climbing walls (53 feet), and one of the longest collegiate fitness tracks in the nation. The whole 264,000-square foot structure was designed by Hughes Group Architects and Brailsford & Dunlavey to be a city unto itself, accommodating a plethora of physical activities, services, sports, and social gatherings. The $53-million building layout is interlaced with sightlines and punctuated with visuals of the various accoutrements seen from every interior point. Visual connections to the University's campus and the Houston skyline entertain the eye throughout the building. As they say, "Ain't nothin' ever easy." Constructing the mammoth center in a climate of extreme heat and humidity, monsoon-sized rains, and the poor geology continually challenged the architects, engineers, and builders. "…but what is truly remarkable," says Dr. Kathleen A. Anzivino, Director of Campus Recreation, "is that the project was completed within the University's original budget and timeframe and has exceeded everyone's expectations."

Above: 28-lane, 70-meter pool.

Right: 53-foot climbing wall.

Opposite upper left: Exterior on long axis.

Opposite left: Basketball court.

Opposite lower left: Quarter-mile fitness track.

Photography: Timothy Hursley.

The first thing students see when they approach the 138,000-square foot landmark Student Recreation Center at the University of North Texas is the multitude of physical activities showcased through its huge windows, which was exactly the design objective of the architect, F&S Partners, Inc., to make the building as open and inviting as possible. Inside the $24.4-million center, warm colors and open spaces encourage students to participate in a three-court basketball gymnasium, a combination basketball/soccer gymnasium, both competition and leisure pools, spa, weight/fitness rooms, and a 45-foot rock climbing wall. "Since the interior is organized around a large, two-story central space, it is exciting to see all of the major activities clearly visible," reports Sue Delmark, CRSS, Assistant Dean and Director of Recreational Sports. The design is a contextual building that complements the university's master plan and surrounding buildings. The subtle brick banding, glass color and metal panels meld with the materials used throughout the campus.

Above: Students reach for the sky 45 feet up.

Opposite above: The open facility invites patrons in.

Opposite below left: A four-lane track circles the interior.

Opposite below right: An 8-lane competitive pool.

Photography: Craig Blackmon, FAIA.

✝NIRSA Outstanding Sports Facilities Awards 2004

University of South Carolina
Strom Thurmond Wellness & Fitness Center
Columbia, South Carolina

Classy, stately, grand: These words spring to mind when going through the large, white, columned entrance of the Strom Thurmond Wellness & Fitness Center at the University of South Carolina. Designed by Cannon Design and the Boudreaux Group, the 192,000-square foot facility combines the best qualities of both a student union and a fitness center, while reflecting the classical architectural style of the University's original 1800's construction. Once inside, patrons enter a rotunda reminiscent of the U.S. Capitol, in keeping with the building's namesake, the nation's longest serving U.S. Senator. With the brilliant overhead dome, the $41.3-million facility is an exciting combination of classical architecture, cutting-edge technology and practical functionality. The use of skylights, open space, wide windows, galleries and corridors throughout adds to the synergy of the Center, plus allows easy supervision of all of its activities. "The Center is a new flagship building for the University," says Herbert Camp, Director of Campus Recreation.

Above right: Rock climbing wall.

Above left: Exterior.

Left: Weight/cardio room.

Lower left: Basketball court.

Opposite: Lobby.

Photography: Rion Rizzo, Creative Resources Photography.

⚡NIRSA Outstanding Sports Facilities Awards 2004

University of Texas Southwestern Medical Center
Bryan Williams, M.D. Student Center
Dallas, Texas

Limited available space and funding were two design challenges for the 45,400-square foot addition to the Bryan Williams, M.D. Student Center at the University of Texas Southwestern Medical Center. However, F&S Partners, Inc. and design consultant Tom Dison produced a very creative layout for a dynamic facility that efficiently uses the available area, yet allows expansion for a pool. The new $8-million addition to the 35-year-old Skillern Student Union allows 1,600 students and 9,000 scientists and physicians to break for physical activities that exemplify the Medical Center's commitment to fitness, sports and lifestyle management.
The finishes for the facility reflect a classic design.

The warm rich tones of the color palette are a sharp contrast to the spartan areas of the hospital campus. An inviting color scheme of rich tones contributes to the dramatic experience of warmth and tranquility, giving the Center its own character. "The Bryan Williams, M.D. Student Center provides a place for students to congregate, interact, learn and enjoy a sense of campus community," says Suzette Smith, CRSS, Director of Facility Operations.

Above right: Cardio room overlooks campus.

Above left: Exterior with Dallas skyline.

Left: Suspended jogging track.

Opposite: Lounge invites physicians and students.

Photography: Craig Blackmon, FAIA.

 **NIRSA** Outstanding Sports Facilities Awards 2004

Western Washington University
Wade King Student Recreation Center
Bellingham, Washington

Since opening in September 2003, the new 98,000-square foot Wade King Student Recreation Center has doubled as a dynamic, inviting and state-of-the-art athletic facility that creates a friendly, accessible and sustainable gathering place for the new south academic core of the Western Washington University campus. The $17.5-million, LEED-certified facility, designed by architect Opsis Architecture with executive architect BJSS Duarte Bryant, nestles into a wooded hillside, capturing dramatic mountain views to the east, as well as to the track and field to the north. "Sustainability was a big factor in the design," reports Marie C. Sather, Director of Campus

Recreational services. Its diversified mix of programs serves a wide range of individual and group recreational activities. For example, the natatorium, comprising a six-lane lap swim and leisure pool as well as a spa, accommodates intramurals, sport clubs, student organizations, and the general student population. In addition, there is a three-court gymnasium with elevated running track, multipurpose activity court, locker rooms and several multipurpose rooms for aerobics, martial arts, yoga and fencing. WWU students, faculty and staff finally have a place to drop in, work out and socialize without being interrupted by other scheduled events on campus.

Above left: Exterior.
Above right: Rock climbing.
Left: Café.
Below left: Gymnasium.
Opposite: Pool.
Photography: Robin Tedder.

✓ NIRSA Outstanding Sports Facilities Awards 2002

Christopher Newport University
The Freeman Center
Newport News, Virginia

When architects Marcellus, Wright, Cox & Smith and Cannon Design created the 112,580-square foot Freeman Center at Christopher Newport University, they designed it with brick and slate on the exterior to harmonize architecturally with the rest of the university campus. Great care was taken so the height of the arena roof and the height of the entrance tower did not overpower the adjacent four-story administrative building. With tall windows placed on two walls, the airy, L-shaped fitness area has three distinct areas, including cardio, weights and circuit training. The $14.8-million facility has a 2,500-seat competition basketball arena and court, and 200-meter, six-lane jogging track. School colors of blue and silver and a three-sail school logo are used throughout the building.

The interior is accented with a blue inlaid terrazzo floor, dramatic canvas sails flutter over the Captain's Café, and bright, bold colors highlight the climbing wall. "The Freeman Center is a striking facility from the moment you step foot inside," says Douglas R. Shipley, Director. "Careful detail was used in this aesthetically pleasing, yet very functional multipurpose facility."

Top left: Basketball court.
Upper left: Fitness room.
Lower left: Café.
Bottom left: Exterior.
Opposite: Reception area.
Photography: Wildman Photography.

NIRSA Outstanding Sports Facilities Awards 2002

Georgia State University
Student Recreation Center
Atlanta, Georgia

Top: Exterior at night.

Left: Terrazzo tile is used throughout.

Above: An eight-lane, 25-yard lap pool with a water vortex.

Opposite: Squash court and exercise room.

Photography: Sam Fentress.

Architects at KPS Group and Hastings & Chivetta Architects, Inc., took Georgia State University's directive to design the $29.5-million Student Recreation Center in downtown Atlanta to be unlike any other building on campus and ran with it. The result: 161,112 square feet of sleek yet dynamic space that also incorporates low maintenance in a fun place! Durable and aesthetically pleasing finishes are achieved both on the interior and exterior by using clear glazing, fiber cement board, smooth aluminum panels, and corrugated, pre-finished metal cladding. While the major interior finish material is ground face CMU, metal railings and elevated walkways are accented with maple panels. The aquatics center, locker room and restrooms feature gray ceramic tile floors and phenolic resin lockers and ceiling mounted partitions. "Transparency throughout the building was rigorously pursued," says Scott R. Levin, CRSS, Director of University Recreation. "As a result, a visitor can see virtually every activity offered by the program from the entry lobby."

Fort Lewis College
Student Life Center
Durango, Colorado

When the students voted to approve the funds to build a new $7.5-million Student Life Center at Fort Lewis College in Durango, Colorado, they insisted on a sustainable facility, both in terms of design and maintenance. Architects Sink Combs Dethlefs and Design Balance Consultants created a 49,632-square foot facility that not only minimizes long-term impacts on the environment, it lowers the long-term energy use and maintenance costs. Building materials are made from an unconventional assortment of recycled products including: countertops made from soybeans and recycled newspapers, cabinet faces from corn husks and wood chips, benches and shelving from recycled milk jugs, locker room tiles from recycled windshields, and wood flooring certified as sustainably harvested. Exterior landscaping features natural plants that are drought resistant and require minimal maintenance. The result is a sustainable facility that promotes health and wellness through non-harmful materials, better ventilation and overall better indoor air quality, yet still provides all of the first-class recreational amenities. "It's a very popular building on campus," says Jack Krider, Director of Recreational Services.

Above: Drought resistant landscaping promotes sustainability.

Right: Suspended jogging track.

Below right: Climbing wall.

Opposite: Special photocells regulate light.

Photography: Laurie Dickson.

❯NIRSA Outstanding Sports Facilities Awards 2002

Loyola Marymount University
Fritz B. Burns Recreation Center
Los Angeles, California

In keeping with Loyola Marymount University's philosophy and heritage, the Jesuit principle of "Development of the whole person," was a keystone for architects Cannon Design when it designed the $18-million Fritz B. Burns Recreation Center. Faced with limited site size, budget constraints, and a criteria that the exterior finish must reflect a classic look to blend with the existing athletic arena, the modern 85,000-square foot facility uses a material palette of glass, metal roofing and exterior plaster. The interior has a large, open, inviting floor with plenty of natural lighting. One of the more creative technical features is the 46-foot x 200-foot Galleria that connects the existing Events Center to the new Recreation Center. Its dramatic floating roof, dominated by a large translucent skylight, has a distinctive visual appeal, creating a major gathering place for athletic, social and cultural events. "The Fritz B. Burns Recreation Center has completely changed the culture at LMU. It makes a dramatic statement while providing increased recreational opportunities to the LMU community," reports Trey Duval, CRSS, Director of University Recreation.

Above right: Pool.
Above left: Building exterior.
Far left: Walkway.
Left: Weight/cardio room.
Below: Gymnasium.
Opposite: Exterior.
Photography: Tom Bonner Photography.

Loyola College in Maryland
Fitness and Aquatic Center
Baltimore, Maryland

One of the considerations that architects Sasaki Associates, Inc. and the Aquatic Design Group had in designing the $21.6-million Fitness and Aquatic Center at Loyola College in Maryland was to create easy second floor access for the 500-plus spectators of the swim meets so as not to disturb participants in the other physical activities. The extremely efficient design, with its small but aesthetically pleasing lobby, allows spectators access to the pool and Café/Eatery without passing through the secured control point. Colorful floor patterns in the carpet are used as directional devices. The exterior of Butler stone complements the Gothic style of the main campus. Polished block, brushed aluminum, and maple wood railings accent the 115, 154-square foot facility's interior, giving it a light and energetic feel appropriate for the Center's purpose. "The Fitness and Aquatic Center is a popular destination for as many as 800 students per day," reports Pamela Wetherbee-Metcalf, Director of University Recreation.

Above: Exterior stone façade matches campus.

Right: Jogging track above basketball court.

Below: Exercise room.

Bottom right: Café.

Opposite: Atrium.

Photography: Greg Hursley & Maxwell Mackenzie.

Kent State University
Student Recreation and Wellness Center
Kent, Ohio

Locally dubbed "The Spike," this striking architectural feature draws 2,000 patrons a day into a three-story, state-of-the-art Student Recreation and Wellness Center at Kent State University. Architect, The Collaborative, Inc. with consultant Hastings & Chivetta Architects, Inc., created this $25-million, 153,000-square foot visually dynamic facility to provide a wide array of wellness and recreation opportunities: a gym for hockey and indoor soccer, sports arena, four racquetball and handball courts, natatorium, 12-rope climbing wall, running track, cardio/weight rooms, pro shop and wellness suite. The airy natatorium contains a six-lane, 25-meter lap pool, leisure pool with hot tub, instructional pool, sauna, waterfall and "lazy river." Security is of foremost importance. The entire facility is viewable from the access mall and a digital system with 30 closed-circuit TVs monitor every area. "The SRWC provides the Kent State University campus with an outstanding facility that greatly adds to the level of satisfaction of students, faculty, staff and local community members," says Dr. Paul Milton, Director of Recreational Services.

Above left: Lazy River swimming pool.

Above: Summit Street Café welcomes patrons.

Left: 12-rope rock climbing wall.

Opposite: "The Spike" dominates the exterior.

Photography: Sam Fentress.

NIRSA Outstanding Sports Facilities Awards 2002

University of Minnesota, Twin Cities
St. Paul Gymnasium Renovation
St. Paul, Minnesota

During its $8-million renovation of the St. Paul Gymnasium at the University of Minnesota, Twin Cities, the goal for architect Stageberg Beyer Sachs, Inc. and consultant Meyer, Borgman, and Johnson, Inc. was to create a functional, modern facility within an historic facade. The patterns in the butter-yellow glazed concrete block on the building's exterior approximate the common brick and buff-colored tile details of the original building, bringing the new and old together. Both the addition and renovation have respected and enhanced the natural lighting with the sky lit connecting gallery and pool, which incorporates five large windows that allow views of the beautifully wooded site. The 56,000-square foot St. Paul Gymnasium now houses a gymnasium, three fitness equipment areas, a jogging track, four racquetball/handball courts, two multipurpose rooms, an 8-lane, 25-yd. pool, and an indoor rock climbing & bouldering area. "The most charming and effective aspect of the building is the use of natural light, and generous windows facing the elegantly arched south-facing front porch," reports Dr. James C. Turman, CRSS, Assistant Vice Provost for Student Affairs and Director for Recreational Sports.

Above: North exterior end with pool addition.

Opposite above right: 8-lane, 25-yard pool.

Opposite below left: Basketball court.

Opposite below right: Corridor.

Photography: Dana Wheelock.

NIRSA Outstanding Sports Facilities Awards 2002

Washington State University
Student Recreation Center
Pullman, Washington

At 160,000-square feet, the Student Recreation Center at Washington State University is the largest of its kind in the Pacific Northwest. The $39-million open, transparent design, by architects Yost Grube Hall and Cannon Design, has gained national attention for its innovative spatial relationships, environmental responsibility, and energy efficiency. Altogether, 25 specific areas use sustainable design, such as high-performance windows, natural ventilation, clerestories that maximize day lighting,

seasonal on-site rainwater retention pond, recycled building materials, finishes of natural stone and wood materials, and recycled rubber for fitness athletic floors. Each day, more than 3,000 students and residents of nearby Pullman, Washington, use the three multipurpose rooms for fitness classes, 200 pieces of cardiovascular and other specialized machines, seven basketball/volleyball/badminton/roller hockey/indoor soccer courts, and the four-lane elevated track.

"The Center demonstrates

the character of the student community, the outstanding use of the site and building materials, and the project's primary design objectives," says Kathleen Hatch, CRSS, Director of University Recreation.

Above: Jogging track, spinning room, gym/basketball courts.

Right: Entire facility seen from lobby.

Opposite above left: Swimming pool.

Photography: David Horsley.

West Virginia University
Student Recreation Center
Morgantown, West Virginia

Striking a balance between aesthetics and function, West Virginia University's Student Recreation Center was designed by architects Moody-Nolan, Inc. and Brailsford & Dunlavey. Their challenge? Fit a multi-story building onto a tight sloping site. Inside, the focal point of the $33.8-million structure is a 50-foot rock climbing wall that soars through the three-leveled facility. The 170,000-square foot center includes weight/fitness equipment, courts for basketball, volleyball, badminton, squash, and racquetball, six-lane pool and leisure pools, 20-seat whirlpool, elevated jogging track and an outdoor area where students can rent ski and camping equipment.

The curved metal roof reflects the campus's overall master plan and ties the structure together inside and out. Throughout the building, sweeping curves are incorporated into many of its design elements, art, carpet and pool shape. "The Student Recreation Center is a striking gateway structure on campus that improves the quality of university community life through recreational activity in an efficient, user-friendly facility," says David H. Taylor, Director of the Student Recreation Center.

Above: Circles in Café carpet.

Top left: Exterior.

Left: Jogging track circles 50-foot rock wall.

Bottom left: Circles in pool design.

Opposite: Glass circles enhance lobby.

Photography: Michael Houghton.

The Designer Series

Visual Reference Publications, Inc.

302 Fifth Avenue, New York, NY 10001
Tel: 212.279.7000 • Fax: 212.279.7014
www.visualreference.com

NIRSA Knows
Recreational Sports Facilities

Plan now! Nationwide, construction of recreational sports facilities on college campuses will continue to grow for years to come.

NIRSA, a non-profit membership organization, directly impacts millions of people and accesses an international network of more than 4,000 highly trained professionals, individuals, and institutional members on university campuses. NIRSA members are managing the complex, high-tech facilities you build. To that end, we offer the following facility-specific resources and advanced educational opportunities.

- **Expo at the NIRSA Annual Conference,** a forum for campus decision makers, architects and designers to come together, network and share ideas.

- **Annual Recreational Sports Facility Construction survey,** an update on construction projects at NIRSA institutions.

- **National Recreation Facilities Institute,** an annual in-depth symposium on the planning, construction, renovation, and operation of recreational sports facilities.

- **Outstanding Sports Facilities Awards,** a showcase of the best in facilities architecture, design and construction.

For more information about NIRSA and membership, please visit our Web site at nirsa.org or call us at 541-766-8211.

NIRSA
www.nirsa.org

NATIONAL INTRAMURAL-RECREATIONAL SPORTS ASSOCIATION
The leading resource for professional and student development, education, and research in collegiate recreational sports.

Index by Project

American Airlines Center, Dallas, TX, **46**

Ameriquest Field / The Ballpark in Arlington, Arlington, TX, **44**

Asphalt Green AquaCenter, New York, NY, **38**

Berkeley High School, Student Union and Recreation Center, Berkeley, CA, **54**

Boardwalk Hall, Atlantic City, NJ, **70**

Boca Rio Golf Club, Boca Raton, FL, **110**

Boise State University, Student Recreation Center, Boise, ID, **146**

Boston College, Yawkey Athletics Center, Chestnut, Hill, MA, **12**

Boston University, Fitness and Recreation Center and Agganis Arena, Boston, MA, **28**

Braga Stadium, Braga, Portugal, **130**

Bucknell University, Kenneth G. Langone Athletic & Recreation Center, Lewisburg, PA, **62**

Chatham College, Athletics & Fitness Center, Pittsburgh, PA, **84**

Christopher Newport Unversity, The Freeman Center, Newport News, VA, **170**

Citizens Bank Park, Philadelphia, PA, **66**

The College of New Jersey, Brower Student Center and Event Center, Ewing, NJ, **102**

Crunch Fitness, Lincoln Park, Chicago, IL, **32**

Disney's Wide World of Sports, Walt Disney World Resort, Lake Buena Vista, FL, **48**

Dr Pepper / 7-Up Ballpark, Frisco, TX, **42**

Duncaster Wellness Center, Bloomfield, CT, **60**

Equinox 54th Street, New York, NY, **108**

Equinox Scarsdale, Scarsdale, NY, **106**

Ford Field Stadium, Detroit, MI, **119**

Fort Lewis College, Student Life Center, Durango, CO, **176**

George Mason University, Aquatic and Fitness Center, Fairfax, VA, **92**

George Mason University, Athletics & Recreation Master Plan, Fairfax, VA, **72**

Georgia Institute of Technology, Campus Recreation Center, Atlanta, GA, **82, 148**

Georgia State University, Student Recreation Center, Atlanta, GA, **174**

The Heights Community Center, Richmond Heights, MO, **78**

Home Depot National Training Center at California State University, Dominguez Hills, CA, **116**

Hudson River Park, Pier 96 Boathouse, New York, NY, **40**

Johns Hopkins University, Ralph S. O'Connor Recreation Center, Baltimore, MD, **122**

Kent State University, Student Recreation and Wellness Center, Kent, OH, **182**

KeySpan Park, Coney Island, Brooklyn, NY **98**

Livonia Community Recreation Center, Livonia, MI, **20**

The Lodge Des Peres, Des Peres, MO, **76**

Loyola College, Fitness and Aquatic Center, Baltimore, MD, **124, 180**

Loyola Marymount University, Fritz B. Burns Recreation Center, Los Angeles, CA, **178**

Monmouth University, Multi-Use Activity Center, West Long Branch, NJ, **58**

Morgan Hill Aquatic Center, Morgan Hill, CA, **52**

Nassau County Aquatics Center, East Meadow, NY, **34**

The Natatorium Community Recreation and Wellness Center, City of Cuyahoga Falls, Cuyahoga Falls, OH, **22**

Noble & Greenough School, Morrison Athletic Center, Dedham, MA, **16**

Old Dominion University, Ted Constant Convocation Center, Norfolk, VA, **114**

Oklahoma State University, Colvin Recreation Center, Stillwater, OK, **150**

Oregon State University, Dixon Recreation Center, Corvallis, OR, **152**

Paul Derda Recreation Center, City and County of Broomfield, Broomfield, CO, **18**

Rec-Plex, St. Peters, MO, **80**

Riverplex, Peoria, IL, **74**

RiverWinds Community Center, West Deptford Township, NJ, **24**

Sonoma State University, Student Recreation Center, Rohnert Park, CA, **154**

Stanford University, Avery Aquatic Center, Stanford, CA, **50**

St. Paul's School, Athletic and Fitness Center, Concord, NH, **10**

Texas Christian University, Student Recreation Center, Fort Worth, TX, **30, 158**

Tradition Field, Port St. Lucie, FL, **104**

Trinity University, Center for Women and Girls Sports, Washington, DC, **96**

University of Alabama, Student Recreation Center, Tuscaloosa, AL, **144**

University of California Santa Barbara, Recreation Center and Aquatic Complex, Santa Barbara, CA, **126**

University of Central Florida, Recreation and Wellness Center, Orlando, FL, **160**

University of Central Oklahoma, Recreation & Wellness Center, Edmond, OK, **86**

University of Houston, Campus Recreation & Wellness Center, Houston, TX, **90, 162**

University of Massachusetts, Lowell, Campus Recreational Center, Lowell, MA, **14**

University of Minnesota, Twin Cities, St. Paul Gymnasium Renovation, St. Paul, MN, **184**

University of North Texas, Student Recreation Center, Denton, TX, **164**

University of Pennsylvania, Pottruck Health and Fitness Center, Philadelphia, PA, **36**

University of South Carolina, Strom Thurmond Wellness & Fitness Center, Columbia, SC, **26, 166**

University of Texas Southwestern Medical Center, Bryan Williams, M.D. Student Center, Dallas, TX, **168**

University of Tulsa, Fulton and Susie Collins Fitness Center, Tulsa, OK, **88**

University of Virginia, Aquatic & Fitness Center, Charlottesville, VA, **94, 156**

USTA National Tennis Center, Flushing,NY, **120**

Van Andel Arena, Grand Rapids, MI, **118**

Washington State University, Student Recreation Center, Pullman, WA, **186**

West Virginia University, Student Recreation Center, Morgantown, WV, **188**

Western Washington University, Wade King Student Recreation Center, Bellingham, WA, **170**